HARDPRESS.NET
HOME OF HARD-TO-FIND BOOKS

The Cambrian Directory
by Cliff (Of Worcester.)

Address:
HardPress
8345 NW 66TH ST #2561
MIAMI FL 33166-2626
USA
Email: info@hardpress.net

gh — Wiles (5

THE

CAMBRIAN DIRECTORY.

—>◆<—

Boards, 4s. 6d.

Gough – Wales 65.

THE

CAMBRIAN DIRECTORY,

OR,

CURSORY SKETCHES

OF THE

WELSH TERRITORIES.

WITH A CHART,

Comprehending at one View,

The advisable Route—Best Inns—Distances—and Objects most worthy of Attention.

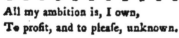

Authors, you know, of greatest fame,
Thro' modesty suppress their name ;
And, wou'd you wish me to reveal
What these superior Wits conceal?
- - - - - - - - - - -
- - - - - - - - - - -
All my ambition is, I own,
To profit, and to please, unknown.

Visions in Verse.

Salisbury:

Printed and sold by J. Easton, High-street: Sold also by T. Hurst, Pater-Noster-Row, *London*; L. Bull, and J. Barratt, *Bath*; J. Norton, and W. Brown, *Bristol*; and O. Tudor, *Monmouth*.

1800.

TO THE

FRIENDLY AND TRULY HOSPITABLE

INHABITANTS

OF THE

PRINCIPALITY OF WALES,

THESE

Cursory Sketches,

ARE RESPECTFULLY

AND GRATEFULLY DEDICATED, BY

The Autho

TO THE

INHABITANTS

OF THE

PRINCIPALITY OF WALES.

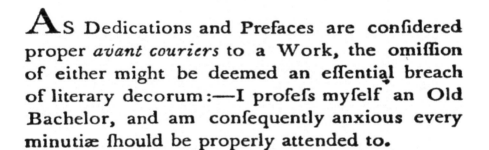

As Dedications and Prefaces are confidered proper *avant couriers* to a Work, the omiffion of either might be deemed an effential breach of literary decorum:—I profefs myfelf an Old Bachelor, and am confequently anxious every minutiæ fhould be properly attended to.

It is generally cuftomary in Dedications, to folicit the patronage of an individual; but, as thefe *Curfory Sketches* will fully prove, I by no means always purfue the common beaten track,

truft

truſt it will not be thought too preſumptious, addreſſing myſelf to *Pluralities*, and humbly requeſting permiſſion, that the CAMBRIAN DIRECTORY may be looked upon as a Ward of the Welſh in general: for I can with ſafety affirm, in no country will the Touriſt experience more true hoſpitality and friendly attention, than in the Principality of Wales: I therefore with true reſpect and gratitude, beg leave to ſubſcribe myſelf,

GENTLEMEN,

Your much obliged

And moſt obedient

Humble ſervant,

THE AUTHOR.

PRE-

PREFACE.

FAULTS, in the following Work, I readily allow, there are many, many; but, flatter my_self, thofe who are beft able to difcover, will be moft ready to pardon them. Tours or Journals, are now hackneyed fubjects; and though this may be confidered as a trite apology, and (if I may fo exprefs myfelf) an Author's loop-hole, yet I can moft truly affert, the prefent Obfervations were by no means at firft, ever intended to be fcanned by the public eye; but merely for my own private amufement, as a memento, to have accefs to, when I wifhed to breathe delight from Recollection's power; my Remarks, therefore, were only fuch as any Traveller, an admirer of Nature, would with a pencil briefly put down; and I muft beg leave again to repeat, I had not then the moft diftant

thought

thought of appearing at the bar of the Public: on my return, I naturally placed my Obfervations in a more connected form; and *fome time afterwards,* accidentally converfing with my Bookfeller, on the romantic beauties of Wales, and fhewing him a few of my Notes, was perfuaded to prepare them for the prefs; in confequence of which, I am now embarking on the literary ocean; and, as a candid behaviour ought to be preferred to all other confiderations, before I fail on my cruize, beg leave to declare, that it is not the intention of the following fheets, either to rival the lively and impreffive defcriptions of a WYNDHAM or a WARNER,—to contend with the literary and hiftorical anecdotes of a PENNANT,—or to equal the mineralogical ftudies of an AIKIN: and here I candidly acknowledge, when attempting a defcription of Monmouthfhire, I found myfelf not a little intimidated, by the intended, and anxioufly expected publication of that county, by a Gentleman,* highly claffed in the literary world,

* The Rev. WILLIAM COXE, rector of Bemerton, and domeftic chaplain to the Lord Bifhop of Salifbury.

for

for many celebrated productions; confcious of my own inability to do ample juftice to that picturefque county, and particularly the rich fcenery of the Wye, when it is already in fuch able hands: I beg from true refpect and efteem, to apply to him the following paffage:

Oh, while along the ftream of time, thy name
Expanded flies, and gathers all its fame,
Say, fhall my little bark attendant fail,
Purfue the triumph, and partake the gale?

POPE.

The CAMBRIAN DIRECTORY, is therefore given to the Public, as a *common Itinerary;* nor does it prefume to have difcovered any thing unknown to the fage Antiquarian,—the deep Mineralogift,—and the buftling Traveller: ftill, however, the Author flatters himfelf, it may be fo far ufeful to the Public, that the Traveller will find it a convenient Pocket Companion; it will tell him the *beft Inns,* and lay before him in one view, the *diftances;* the Mineralogift may occafionally learn, what Rocks will moft deferve his attention; and it will point out to the

Anti-

Antiquarian, every venerable Ruin, that feems
to tell the religious or military hiftory of the
country. Such is the " plain unvarnifh'd tale:"
in addition to which, I folicit permiffion to ad-
drefs my Readers with a line from a favourite
Author :

" Laugh where you *Muft*, be candid where you *Can.*"

THE

THE

CAMBRIAN DIRECTORY.

THESE ARE THE HAUNTS OF MEDITATION, THESE
THE SCENES WHERE ANCIENT BARDS TH' INSPIRING BREATH
EXTATIC FELT !

Thomſon.

TWO Friends, equally admirers of Nature's land-
ſcapes, and attached to pedeſtrian independence, agreed
to viſit the wild and impreſſive ſcenery of the Cambrian
Mountains ; and the outlines of their Route being arranged, ſallied forth in the month of July, 1798, from

CHELTENHAM,

a place much reſorted to during the ſummer months,
and celebrated for its Mineral Waters, is compoſed of

B   one

one ftreet, in almoft a ftraight line, nearly the length
of a mile. Since it has become a place of fafhion,
the lodging houfes have been confiderably improved,
and rendered comfortable for the company, who make
this place their fummer refidence. The feafon ufually
commences about May, and frequently continues till
the beginning of November. The majority of the
company who frequent Cheltenham, refort here not fo
much for the purpofe of water-drinking, as to enjoy
the delightful walks and rides, and partake of the
fociability of the neighbourhood.

The Walk at the Pump-room, well planned, and
kept in excellent order, is planted on each fide with
limes; at the end is a fmall fquare, where the Pump is
fituate, with a room on the left for the accommodation
of the company to promenade, meafuring fixty-fix feet
by twenty-three;—on the oppofite fide a reading-
room, with a billiard-table over, and a houfe, the refidence of the attendant at the Spa; beyond that, is a
fimilar walk of three hundred and twelve feet, which
leads to another ferpentine walk; from the end of this,
the Spire of Cheltenham Church forms a beautiful
object. Near thefe walks, ftands, on an eminence, the
Seat of the Earl of Fauconberg: this was the Royal
refidence during their Majefties ftay at this place, from
July 12th to Auguft 16, 1788.

In

In refpeƈt to the rides, Cleave-hill, Dowdefwell, &c. Tewkefbury and Gloucefter, are moſt admired.

Speaking of the Hiſtory of the place, we find Cheltenham was a town in the reign of William the Conqueror : Edward likewiſe is fuppofed to have marched through it, before he encamped his army on the field of Tewkeſbury, previous to the battle of the Houfes of York and Lancaſter.

Of the efficacy of the Water, to which this town is indebted for its prefent celebrity, I refer my readers to a Treatiſe, publiſhed by Dr. Fothergill, of Bath.

GLOUCESTER.

The Pin Manufaƈtory was eſtabliſhed here, by John Tiſley, in the year 1626, and the bufinefs is now become ſo extenſive, that the returns from London alone are eſtimated at near 20,000*l. per ann.* Before the introduƈtion of Pins into England (1543) ſkewers of brafs, ſilver, and gold, and likewiſe thorns curiouſly ſcraped, called by the Welch women *pin-draen,* were uſed. Though the Pins themſelves are apparently ſimple, yet their manufaƈture is not a little curious and complex. The wire in its moſt rough ſtate is brought

B 2

from

from a wire company in the neighbourhood of Briftol:
till the year 1563, Englifh iron wire was drawn out by
manual ftrength.   The firft operation attending. this
curious procefs, is the fixing the circular roll of wire to
the circumference of a wheel, which in its rotation
throwing the wire againft a board, with great violence,
takes off the black external coat: vitriol is next applied
to bring the brafs to its common colour.   The brafs
wire being too thick for the purpofe of being cut into
Pins, is reduced to any dimenfion the workman pleafes,
by forcibly drawing it through an orifice in a fteel
plate, of a fmaller diameter.   The wire, being thus
reduced to its proper dimenfions, is next ftraightened :
it is then cut into portions of fix inches in length, and
afterwards to the fize of the Pin, and each piece refpec-
tively fharpened on a grinding-ftone, turned by a wheel.
We now come to a diftinct branch of the manufactory :
the forming the heads, or, as the workmen term it,
head fpinning : this is accomplifhed by means of a
fpinning-wheel, which, with aftonifhing rapidity winds
the wire round a fmall rod: this, when drawn out,
leaves a hollow tube between the circumvolutions;
every two circumvolutions, or turns, being cut with
fheers, form one head.   The heads, thus formed, are
diftributed to children, who, with great dexterity, by
the affiftance of an anvil, or hammer, worked by the
foot, fix the point and the head together.   The Pins,
                                                    thus

thus formed, are boiled in a copper, containing a folution of block-tin pulverized, and the lees of Port; and by this laft procefs, it changes its yellow brafſy colour, and aſſumes the appearance of filver, or tin. The labourers are all paid according to the weight of their work.

Near Gloucefter, at the fmall ifland of Alney, formed by the river Severn, hiftorians relate, that Canute and Edmund, after many bloody engagements in Eſſex, determined to prevent a farther effufion of blood by a fingle combat. Neither, however, as the ftory relates, obtaining a victory, peace was concluded, and the kingdom divided between them. We paid, however, little regard to the fuppofed place of this conteft, as it was not for us, puifne antiquarians, to difcufs points, on which the greateft hiftorians had fo materially differed.

I forbear to make any remarks on the Cathedral and Gaol of Gloucefter, as much has already been done towards their illuftration; and as ample accounts of them are given in the Gloucefter Guide, which the Tourift will meet with on the fpot.

The Walk from hence to

WEST-

WESTBURY,

is by no means uninterefting; the country is ftudded with half-feen villas, and animated with churches, whilft the retrofpect commands a fine view of Robinhood's Hill, with the dark Tower of Gloucefter Cathedral, juft rifing in the perfpective.

At Weftbury is the Seat of Maynard Colchefter, Efq. The Church, with a detached Spire, ftands clofe to the houfe. Near this place mineralogifts will be highly gratified by vifiting a Cliff, called *Garden*, or *Golden Cliffe*; which is moft beautifully encrufted with mundic and cryftals. This rock, ftanding clofe to the Severn, is only acceffible at the reflux of the tide; and when illuminated by the fun wears a moft beautiful appearance.

Between Weftbury and Newnham, in an extremely delightful valley, bordering on the Foreft of Deane, is fituate

FLAXLEY ABBEY,

the Seat of Sir Thomas Crawley Bovey. This valley was formerly called *Caftiard*, or the *Happy Valley*; and

and a Monaftery, for Ciftercian Monks, was founded here by Roger, the fecond Earl of Hereford, and the charter confirmed by Henry II. The Abbey was ftanding till the year 1777, when part of it was unfortunately confumed by fire; fince that a confiderable portion of building has been added, and is become a very defirable fummer refidence. The Views from the park, behind the houfe, are very extenfive, commanding the Vale of Gloucefter, and the River Severn, gay with veffels, whilft the extenfive Foreft of Dean, and Flaxley Abbey, form nearer objects for admiration. This wood abounds with the moft charming walks; and, while it affords refrefhing fhelter from a fummer's fun, admits partial views of the adjacent country. Camden, in fpeaking of the Foreft of Dean, derives its name from Ardene, a wood in the Gaulic and Britifh languages. It lies between the two rivers Severn and Wye, and contains thirty thoufand acres. The foil is well adapted for the growth of oaks, and foreft timber; and the fituation particularly commodious for exporting it for fhip-building, and other purpofes. The immenfe quantities of wood annually felled for the ufe of the navy, have fo thinned this wood of its timber, that it is now preferved till a certain growth by act of parliament. Camden obferves, that the oak of this Foreft was fo confiderable, that the Spanifh Armada had orders to

deftroy

deſtroy the timber of it in 1588 : it ſuffered conſidera-
bly in the great rebellion,

The Iron Manufactory has long been carried on in
this Foreſt; and to this day immenſe beds of iron cinders are found, the reliques of the Romans. Theſe
cinders are not half exhauſted of their ore, and are con-
ſequently worked over again : a proof that the Romans
knew only the weak power of the foot blaſt.

As we drew near

NEWNHAM,

the Severn became more conſiderable. The town,
ſituated on the banks of the river, and backed by the
Foreſt of Dean, is very ancient, and in 1018 this manor was granted by King Canute to the Benedictine
Abbey of Perſhore, in Worceſterſhire.*

The Church-yard affords a variety of objects worthy
the attention of the paſſing ſtranger, amongſt which the
Church of Weſtbury forms the moſt conſpicuous feature in the landſcape.

* Atkins's Glouceſterſhire,

The

The View, previous to our defcending the hill to

LIDNEY,

is extenfive and beautiful. In this place Iron Works are carried on by a Mr. Pitchcock.—About a mile from Lidney, the Old Paffage,—King's-road, with the merchant fhips lying off Briftol,— Glouceſterſhire and Somerfetfhire hills, ftudded with gentlemens' feats, churches, and half-feen cottages, formed a chearful landfcape.

CHEPSTOW.

The weather prevented our feeing the celebrated Walks of Piercefield, but we promifed ourfelves the pleafure of vifiting them on our return down the Wye. The Caftle of Chepftow, called Kafwent, or Caftelk Gwent, ftands on a rock wafhed by the river Wye, near its influx into the Severn. Topographical writers differ in their accounts concerning the antiquity of the Caftle, but it is generally fuppofed to have been built at the fame time with the town, appearing at that period to have been a kind of citadel to Chepftow.* The

* Grofe's Antiquities,

Caftle

Caſtle was formerly of great extent, as, according to Leland's account, the " waulles began at the end of " the great bridge over Wy," yet " in the caſtel ys one " tower, as I heard ſay, by the name of Langine." Little now remains of its former grandeur : but, impelled by an irrreſiſtible curioſity, we aſcended the decayed ſteps of the tower, from whence the eye traced with pleaſure the windings of the Wye, till it was at laſt loſt in its conjunction with the Severn. With horror we examined the dark dungeon, where Henry Martin, one of the twelve judges, who ſat to condemn Charles I. was confined ſeven and twenty years.

Grand views of the Briſtol Channel ſtill continued to form intereſting objects from the road; but about three miles from Chepſtow, we turned into ſome fields on the right, to examine the Ivy-mantled walls of

CALDECOT CASTLE.

On our firſt entrance we gazed with that wrapt aſtoniſhment, that fears to diſturb, or be diſturbed by the mutual communication of thought.—Mr. Warner, in his ſurvey of this ruin, was much diſappointed ; but I cannot help allowing, although the view from it was inferior to Chepſtow, yet its antiquated walls wear a
nobler

nobler appearance; and the gloom that reigns around it, forces a figh, and evinces the tranfitory nature of fublunary greatnefs. The antiquity of the building is very obfcure: it is fituate on a flat, and memorable for the birth of Henry VII. Paffing through the village of Caldecot, we foon entered

CAERWENT,

on the Weftern fide, through the broken fragments of its walls, of which one immenfe mafs has recently fallen. This ancient town is now little more than a village, with a few fcattered cottages, but formerly celebrated, under the aufpices of Agricola, for its temples, theatre, porticos, and baths; few veftiges of its former fplendour are now extant. A few fragments of loofe ftones only remain to point out its former extent. In an orchard, adjoining a farm-houfe belonging to Mr. Lewis, is the beautiful teffalated Roman Pavement, difcovered in the year 1777. The tefferale or dies, about an inch in breadth, and half in depth, are nearly cubical, confifting of four colours, red, yellow, blue, and white,* which are ftill in great prefervation; the whole is furrounded with a border, much refembling a Turkey carpet. The daily depre-

* Warner's Firft Walk through Wales.

dations

dations on thefe curious remains of antiquity are greatly
to be lamented.

In the road from Caerwent, amongft other objects
for admiration, the Manfion of Sir Robert Salifbury,
on the left, commanding an extenfive view, attracted
our notice. Paffing through the neat village of Chriftchurch, animated with white-wafhed cottages, and
graced with its fimple Church, which ftands on an
eminence, we left the turnpike road, at the 13th mile
ftone ; and following a footpath through fome fields,
near the banks of the Ufke, foon entered the ancient
city of

CAERLEON,

over a wooden bridge, built on the fome plan as Chepftow. This city was formerly a metropolitan fee, but
St. David, the national faint of Wales, thinking the
noify intercourfe of a populous city, like Caer-Lleon,
ill adapted for contemplation, or the folitary caft of his
mind, removed it to Menevia, which from that period
has been called Ty Dewi by the Welch, and St. David
by the Englifh.*   The remains of its ancient grandeur

---

* He was buried in the Cathedral Church of St. David, and many
hundred years after canonized by Pope Califtus the Second.—*Godwin's
Englifh Bifhops,* p. 414.

are

are ftill difcernible.   Whilft tracing the extent of its
amphitheatre, furrounded by a circular entrenchment,
and the grandeur of its porticoes, we took a retrofpect
on the exertions of man, the fate of kingdoms, and of
rulers; and, marking the grand deftruction of ages, it
feemed to convince us of the tranfientnefs of human
worth and happinefs!   The fhips in the Briftol Channel, with Flat and Steep Holmes rifing in the midft of
the fea, formed pleafing objects in the diftant view,
whilft the mellow green of nearer woods, and meadows
watered by the Ufke, made a combination of hues gay
and beautiful.

Near

NEWPORT

a new ftone bridge is erecting by contract for 10,165*l.*
by Mr. Edwards, fon to the Edwards, who built the
famous Pont y Pridd.   It is to confift of five arches.

Newport Caftle, ftanding on the bank of the river
Ufke, is a fmall diftance from the bridge: it evidently
appears to have been once a place of confiderable extent,
and built for the defence of the paffage over the river;
three ftrong towers commanded the Ufke, but towards
the town a common wall, without any flanks, feems to
have

have been its fole defence.   Some of the windows ftill
remain, the relics of Gothic architecture, and appear
to have been elegantly decorated.   From the tower is a
fine view of the Ufke.   Between Newport and

CARDIFF

we croffed the little ftream of Ebwith, near the park of
Tridegar Houfe, belonging to Sir Charles Morgan.
The grounds are well planned, and command the hills
of Machan and Tombalœ, with the church of Paffanefs
rifing in the centre, on an eminence.   The whole valley, indeed, is prettily fituated.   Paffing through the
villages of Pedifton and Caftletown, we foon reached
the bridge of two arches, over the river Romney, which
divides England from Wales.

The fituation of Cardiff is on a low flat, near the
mouth of the Taafe, over which has lately been thrown
a new Bridge, built by Mr. Parry in 1796 : it confifts
of three large and two fmaller arches.   The tower
of the church is very light, and of elegant workmanfhip;
but nothing in the infide is worthy of infpection.

The Caftle derives its name from the river Taff,
which wafhes its walls ; *Caertaph* fignifying the Town
or

or Caftle upon Taff. Robert Fitzham having conquered Glamorganfhire, divided the country into different portions, among the twelve Norman Knights, as
a reward for their fervice, and took for his own fhare
the Town of Cardiff; and erected, in the year 1110,
this Caftle, in which he generally refided, and held his
court of chancery and exchequer. In the beginning of
May 1645, during the troubles under Charles I. it
was in the poffeffion of the Royalifts, but it was fur-
rendered to Parliament before Auguft 1646.

We entered the Caftle by two ftrong gates, which
ftill remain in great prefervation, but we were difgufted
with the modern architecture of the new-built manfion,
erected by the late Marquis of Bute: the neat fhorn
grafs, the gravel walk, were circumftances that ill accorded with the mutilated walls of an ancient ruin,
which has braved the ftorms of fo many centuries. The
circumftance that tends to render this Caftle a melancholy place in hiftory, is the unjuft confinement of
Robert Duke of Normandy, brother to William Rufus
and Henry I. The accounts, however, of his confinement have been greatly exaggerated by hiftorians; and
a dark vaulted room, beneath the level of the ground,
meafuring nearly a fquare of fifteen feet and a half, is
ftill pointed out as the place of his confinement; a
fmall crevice in the top, about half a yard in length,
and

and three inches wide, was the only place to admit the air. He was buried in Gloucefter Cathedral, where his effigy as big as life, carved in Irifh oak, and painted, is yet fhewn. The Keep, which is ftill very perfect, of an octagon fhape, ftands on an eminence in the centre of a large fquare. Having walked round the ramparts, which command extenfive views of the adjacent country, we vifited the Caftle itfelf, which has, within thefe few years, been repaired, but ftill-remains in an unfinifhed ftate. In the Dining-room are fome portraits, in length, of the Windfor family: the moft ftriking are,

1ft. Sir William, who firft raifed forces for Queen Mary.

2d. Sir Edward, who firft entered the breach at the taking of St. Quintin, in Flanders, where the famous Conftable de Montmorency was taken prifoner.

In the Breakfaft-parlour is a family piece, confifting of feven figures: it was painted in the year 1568. Holbein, I rather imagine, was the painter: it confifts of two Sifters playing at Cards, and two Brothers at Drafts, with Edward Earl of Windfor and his lady looking on. The ftyle is ftiff, with ruffs, fmall black caps and feathers.

Andrew

Andrew Windſor, to the right of the fire-place ; General in the reign of Queen Ann, ſerving in the 28th regiment of foot   - - *Kneller.*

Thomas Windſor, to the left, who ſerved in ſeveral wars of William and Queen Ann, and was Colonel of the 3d regiment of Dragoon Guards, in the reign of George I.   - - - *Kneller.*

Lady Urſula Windſor   - *ibid.*

Hon. Maſter Windſor   - *Painter unknown.*

A good painting of Urſula Counteſs of Windſor, with her grand-daughter Urſula Windſor, *Kneller.*

Thomas Lord Windſor, Governor of Jamaica   - - - - *Vandyke.*

Hon. Charlotta Windſor   - *Dahl.*

Hon. Urſula Windſor   - *Dahl.*

Hon. Dixia Windſor, ſtorekeeper of the ordnance, and for ſix ſucceſſive parliaments member for Cambridge.

This Caſtle belongs to a grandſon of the Marquis of Bute.

In this place, Robert Earl of Glouceſter founded a Priory of White-friars, and another of Black, which continued till the reign of Henry VIII. Only the
C ſhell

fhell of the White-friars is now extant, and the ruins of the Black-friars are inhabited by fifhermen.

From hence we walked to infpect the remains of that once celebrated city

LANDAFF;

the ruins of the old Cathedral are very beautiful, the door cafes are all Norman architecture elegantly mould-ed; two of which, on the North and South fides, are fine fpecimens of that æra. All the other parts are Gothic: the nave is unroofed. Within thefe ruins we entered the Cathedral, which carries with it more the appearance of a modern theatre, than a place of divine worfhip, fo erroneous was the tafte of the architect, in combining with the facred Gothic, a fantaftical work of his own. Among feveral ancient monuments, are two very elegant ones of the Mathews family,* whofe defcendants own the feite of the Bifhop's Caftle, of which only the gate remains : the reft, with the Arch-deacon's houfe, was deftroyed by Owen Glendour.†
There are likewife the monuments of two bifhops, with another, and the figure of Lady Godiva, full length, carved in marble on it. *The wife of John !ō Audley.x*

* Willis's Landaff, p. 34.   † Grofe, Willis.

x Willis p. 22

Landaff

Landaff ſtands on a ſmall eminence, commanding a view of Cardiff, and the ſurrounding country.—We returned again to Cardiff: and the firſt ſix miles of our road to

CAERPHILY

were not very intereſting, till aſcending Thorn Hill, the beauties of the vale below, with Flat and Steep Holmes riſing in the diſtant proſpect, the ruins of Cardiff Caſtle, and the ivy-mantled walls of Landaff Cathedral, amply compenſated for the trouble of climbing this eminence. A little farther on, Caerphily Caſtle burſt upon our ſight, and

———————" ſeem'd to frown,
" In awful majeſty on all around."

The founder, and the time of its erection are very uncertain; but I refer my readers to the firſt volume of the *Archæologia*; to an ingenious Diſſertation, by Daines Barrington, where it is ſatisfactorily proved to have been the work of Edward I. This Caſtle is one of the nobleſt ruins of ancient architecture now remaining in the kingdom, and exceeds all in bigneſs, except that of Windſor. The Hall and the Chapel may ſtill be traced; the former meaſures about ſeventy feet in length, thirty-four in breadth, and ſeventeen in height.

C 2 The

The roof is vaulted about eight feet high, and supported by twenty arches. On the North side is a chimney, ten feet wide, with two windows on each side, extending down to the floor, and carried above the supposed height of this room. At each angle was originally a round tower of four stories, communicating with each other by a gallery. On the West side of the Hall stairs, is a low round tower, of one story, called the Mint-house, with three painted arches on the South side, and a square well on the West. The leaning tower, towards the East end, more particularly engaged our notice : it is divided into two separate parts, by a large fissure, which runs from the top down almost to the middle. Its lineal projection is supposed to be on the outer side, about eleven feet and a half. On the West and North are visible vestiges of a drawbridge. The East wall, on the South side of the principal entrance, is fluted between the buttresses, with battlements on their tops, to protect the intermediate walls.

At Caerphily we perceived a great change in the manners of the people ; in the whole village, scarcely one person was capable of speaking English.

We now came to the celebrated vale of Glamorganshire, so justly styled the *Garden of South-Wales* ; the
rapid

rapid Taafe forms an almost continued uproar for many miles; on the opposite side the mountains rose almost perpendicularly in a massy wall, and sometimes to the water's edge, finely clothed with wood. Every circumstance conspired to heighten the solitary grandeur of the scene, and to prolong the luxurious melancholy, which the views inspired. In this celebrated vale is found the famous Pont y Pridd, or New Bridge, about three quarters of a mile from the Duke of Bridgewater's Arms, a comfortable inn, and far surpassing our miserable quarters at Caerphily. This wonderful bridge, of one arch, is the segment of a circle; the chord of it is one hundred and forty feet, and the heighth of the key-stone, from the spring of the arch, thirty-two feet and a half. It was erected, in the year 1750, by William Edwards, a country mason, who failed in his attempt three times, till, by lightening the abutments, it has resisted, for many years, the torrents of the Taafe.

The intrusion of art in this romantic valley, where nature has been so lavish of her beauties, is much to be lamented: a canal, for the purpose of conveying the iron from the Myther Works to Cardiff, renders it a place of frequent business and confusion; a place originally so well adapted to retirement and reflection.

MY-

MYTHER TIDVIL,

is a moſt miſerable dirty place; the ſoil and the inhabitants both partook of a dark dingy colour : the women
deſtitute of ſhoes and ſtockings, the men and boys the
ſlaves of Vulcan. The Iron-works, under the direction
of Mr. Cramſhaw, are the largeſt in the kingdom; not
leſs than one thouſand hands are employed by this gentleman, who allows the perſon who inſpects the machinery one-eighth of the profits, to keep them in repair. Four large blaſt furnaces, with a number of a
ſmaller ſize, beſides a row of forges, are continually in
uſe. An enormous wheel has lately been conſtructed,
with ſeveral inferior ones, acting in contrary directions,
which pumps the air into a large ſpace, from whence
it is diſtributed, through various tubes, to each ſeparate
furnace. This wheel is fifty feet one inch in diameter,
and ſix feet eight inches in width. The whole weight
reſts on gudgeons, of one hundred tons. The gudgeons
of all the wheels, and of ſuch parts of the machine
where there is any friction, have water continually running over them, to prevent their taking fire. It is the
particular office of one man to greaſe every part of the
machine, whilſt in motion; to accompliſh which, he
is frequently obliged to ride on an iron bar, ſimilar to
the lever of a pump when in motion, a conſiderable

way

way from the ground. The whole of this machinery
is worked by water, not more than a foot deep, which
is conveyed by a long fpout to the top of the wheel,
where it difcharges itfelf. The ore, flux,* and coals,
which they ufe to promote the fufion of the ore, are all
found on the fpot. The ore, previous to its being
thrown into the furnace, is burnt in a common lime-
pit, the goodnefs of it afterwards proved, by its adhefion
to the tongue : the coal is all charked, and continually
put in the furnace, with certain proportions of ore.
From the pigs, the iron is rolled into flat plates by a
cylinder ; this is performed with the greateft difpatch.
The gaunt figures of the workmen excite both pity and
terror, and the fallow countenances and miferable air
of the people, prove it is a labour very prejudicial to
their health. From hence we travelled the road to

PONT NEATH VECHAN,

inacceffible for carriages, indifferent for pedeftrians,
and affording nothing worthy our attention. It lay
over a barren heath, with mountains on one fide, and a
dreary wafte of land before us. About a mile and a
half from Vechan, we unexpectedly defcended through
a wood into a rich romantic valley, watered by Neath

* i. e. lime-ftone.

River.

River.   In this retired fituation we found the Angel
Inn, of Pont Neath Vechan.   Defcription can fcarcely
fuggeft the full grandeur and magnificence of this valley: woods, rocks, and waterfalls, all unite, to render
it *beautiful*.   Our Ciceroni firft conducted us to the
fall of Scotenogam, on the river Purthen, about a mile
and a half from the houfe : this fall we faw to great
advantage, the river having gathered in its courfe the
accumulation] of many torrents after the rain, precipitates itfelf in one majeftic expanfe of water, near
feventy feet high ; whilft the dark lowering rocks, on
each fide, contrafted finely with the varied vegetation
around us.   The defcent is by no means eafy, but the
grandeur of the fcene amply compenfated for all difficulties.   Our Ciceroni next conducted us to a very
inferior one, called the Lady's Cafcade, on the river
Neath ; but of this we caught a very indifferent profpect, the afcent of the mountain being inacceffible, and
the water too high to admit of our obtaining a due infpection of it.   We then returned to our inn, and fet
out a different road, in queft of nature's landfcapes.——
Having walked about three miles, we heard the angry
roar of fmall cafcades; this we confidered as preludes
of fcenes, where the water-fall fwells into a torrent;
and we foon found ourfelves near the fall of Lower
Culhepfte.   The character of this cataract differs very
much from that of Scotenogam; being broken in its
                                        defcent

defcent from projecting rocks, of an immenfe fize.
About a quarter of a mile from hence, we defcended a
rugged and fteep rock to examine the fall of Upper-
Culhepfte, about fifty feet high. The fingularity of
this fall invites the curiofity of the traveller more than
any other in Wales: the whole river precipitates itfelf
with fuch violence, as to leave a fpace between the rock
and the fall fufficiently wide for a horfe path. Though
in lefs than two minutes we were completely wet by
the fpray, yet the effect was awful and fublime; and it
was neceffary to remember the fixed foundation of the
rocks above our heads, to foften the awe they infpired.
Near this fall is Porthogo Cavern, through which the
river Vendre runs. The water was too high to admit
our entrance; our Conductor, however, informed us,
he had penetrated about half a mile, but found the
river wind fo many ways, he judged it fafer to return,
left he fhould fhare the fate of a poor man, who loft
himfelf in this Cavern for the fpace of three days. On
our return, a very intelligent gentleman, ftaying in the
neighbourhood, ftrenuoufly recommended us to defcend
a fteep mountain, on our left, to furvey a curious quad-
rangular ftrata of marble in the rock below. With
fome difficulty we effected our purpofe, having waded
twice through the river. This ftrata in Welch is
called *Bwr Maen*, which fignifies a Stone Bow: it is
fituated clofe to the river Dynnas, which, forcing its

way

way through fome broken fragments of the rock, forms
a cafcade a little above. The price offered for this
grey marble, in London, is fifteen fhillings a foot
fquare.

About five miles from Vechan is the Seat of Mrs.
Holbrow, on the right. We were prevented vifiting
the water-falls of Melincourt and Aperdulas, the river,
owing to the late floods, being too deep to ford. Our
route ftill continued through the valley we had fo much
admired the evening before. As we drew near

NEATH,

the Tower of Knole Caftle had a pleafing effect from a
diftance : it was built by Sir Herbert Mackworth, and
is at prefent in the poffeffion of Lady Mackworth.
The windows from the banqueting-room compre-
hend a circle of many miles diameter, compofed of
Neath Valley and River, with the fmoky Town of
Neath,—the Mumbles Point—Swanfea, and the Channel. The artificial cafcade is well contrived, but,
after the foaming torrents of Scotenogam and Culhepfte, appears very tame.

The fcite of the Refectory, the Chapel, the Hall,
and

and feveral other rooms in the ruins of Neath Abbey, may ftill be traced. It ftands on the Eaft of the river, and was formerly, by Leland's account, the " faireft " abbay of all Wales;" but in his *Collectanea** he feems to give Margam the preference of all the Ciftercian houfes in thefe parts. It was founded for White Monks by Richard Granville. In this Abbey, the unfortunate Edward II. fecreted himfelf till he was taken. Near the ruins are the Copper-works. The ore is chiefly imported from Cornwall, and Wicklow in Ireland; being calcined, and thereby lofing its fulphur, it is refined by the fimple procefs of frequent melting, and taking off the drofs, which forms a fcum; laftly, being moulded into fmall plates, or pigs, it is fhipped for the market. The method of reducing the metal, when melted into fmall particles, is by pouring it into water, and, when thus reduced, it is called *Copper Shot.* Brafs is a compound of copper thus reduced, and *lapis calaminaris,* pulverized in crucibles, and moulded or caft into plates. *Lapis calaminaris* is dug in great quantities near Holywell, in Flintfhire.

The Town of Neath is very unpleafantly fituated, and generally covered with the, fmoke of the Copper-works; a circumftance which I fhould imagine renders

* Vol. ii. p. 92.

it

it an unhealthy fpot.   On that account it is advifable,
both for horfemen and pedeftrians, in their way to
Swanfea, to take the road by Britton Ferry, in preference to the turnpike, which the fmoke always renders
offenfive.

BRITTON FERRY.

This village is much reforted to, on account of its
beautiful fituation ; and many a white-wafhed cottage
ftraggles through the hamlet.   The plantations of
Lord Vernon are well difpofed, and edge the water's
brink : the river is conftantly filled with veffels, whofe
gay ftreamers glittering to the fun-beam, prefent to
the eye a conftant moving object.   Having croffed the
Ferry, we proceeded on the fands to

SWANSEA.

The whole of this walk commanded a boundlefs view
of the ocean to the Weft, whilft to the South the faint
hues of Somerfetfhire coaft fkirted the horizon.

Swanfea is a well-built fea-port town, on the river
Tawe, much reforted to during the fummer months.
The machines for bathing are kept about half a mile
from

from the town, under the direction of Mrs. Landey, who likewise keeps a lodging-house near the place: the charges are twenty-five shillings a week, board and lodging, and ten shillings and six-pence a week for a private parlour. The Castle is supposed to have been erected by Henry Earl of Warwick, in the reign of Henry I.: the small arches round the top of it are exactly similar to the building of Lantphey Castle, and King John's Hall, St. David's, Pembrokeshire. This Castle is now turned into a goal and workhouse. The Market-place is said to be covered with the lead of St. David's Cathedral, given by Cromwell to a gentleman of Swansea.

The clay used for the Pottery, long carried on in this place, is brought from Corfe, in Dorsetshire; having been mixed with finely-ground flint, and dissolved in water, it is passed through sieves, till it has lost all its coarser particles, then exposed to heat, which evaporates the water, and leaves the clay of a consistency sufficient for working. The vessel is first rudely formed by the hand, the clay being stuck to a circular board, which has an horizontal rotation. The other operation consists in the more perfect forming of the work by various processes, and the colouring, glazing, painting, and stamping, drying and baking kilns complete the work.

OYSTER-

OYSTERMOUTH CASTLE,

about five miles from Swanſea, is finely ſituated on an eminence, commanding a delightful proſpect of the ſurrounding country, and the Mumbles' Bay. The ivy-mantled walls of this Caſtle are ſufficiently perfect, to diſtinguiſh what the apartments were originally deſigned for. It formerly belonged to the lords of Gower, but is now in the poſſeſſion of the Duke of Beaufort. Our curioſity being ſatisfied, we haſtened to the

MUMBLES,

celebrated far and near for the goodneſs and abundance of its oyſters. This village ſtands at the extremity of Swanſea Bay, on a vaſt maſs of ſplinter'd rock : from this elevation, the wide expanſe of the ocean and Swanſea Bay are viewed to great advantage. Theſe rocks are inacceſſible at high-water, except in a boat; on the fartheſt is erected a light-houſe.

At Pennard, we deſcended ſome immenſe ſand-banks, which led us into Oxwich Bay : at the head of the ſand-banks are the ſmall remains of an old caſtle,*

* Pennarth, eight miles South-weſt of Swanſea.

ſcarcely

scarcely worthy of observation. The sands in this bay are extremely fine, and the bold projections of the rock exhibit nature in her most awful and impressive attitudes. To the right of Oxwich Bay is situate, at Penrice, the Seat of Mr. Talbot: the grounds are well planned, and command extensive views of the sea: the old Castle rising behind the house gave the whole a fine effect.

Between Penrice and the neat village of

CHERITON,

we observed to our right, on a hill, a large flat stone, several tons weight, resting on about six smaller ones, placed perpendicularly, and standing about five feet high : this is vulgarly called *King Arthur's Stone.* It is here proper to forewarn both Tourists and Travellers, not to fix on Pennard, Penrice, or Cheriton, as places for a night's abode, as they cannot possibly be comfortably accommodated. This advice I mention from experience, for at the latter place, we were under the necessity of contenting ourselves with tables or chairs, as substitutes for beds, and even destitute of necessary provisions. On a hill, opposite our inn, we discovered evident vestiges of a Roman encampment;

from

from this elevation the eye caught a fine view of Carmarthen Bay, and the bold promontory of Worm's Head, to the South-west : this rock is only accessible at low water.

The country through which we traversed for the four or five last miles, is inhabited by a colony of Flemings, who settled here in the reign of Henry I. In the reign of this King's Father, a great number of Flemings, having been driven out of their habitations, by a very extraordinary inundation of the sea, sought protection in England, where they were cordially received. But so many of these people being dispersed in different parts of the kingdom, began, by increase of their numbers, to create some uneasiness ; which Henry I. removed, by settling them as a colony in South Wales, and gave them the country adjoining to Tenby and Haverfordwest. By this wise policy, the King rid his own dominions of an incumbrance, and curbed the insolence of the then rebellious Cambrians.* The little territory they inhabit is called *Gwyr*, and by the English, *Little England beyond Wales*, because their manners and language are still distinguishable from the Welsh, and, in point of speech, assimilate the English. These Flemings, to this day, seldom or never intermarry

* William of Malmsbury, p. 158.

with

with the Welſh : they ſpeak good Engliſh, and are very much averſe to the manners and language of the country they inhabit; both ſexes generally diſtinguiſh themſelves by wearing a ſhort cloak, called *Gowyr Wittle.*

In preference to a long walk, of near thirty miles, we croſſed the River Bury, as the pleaſanteſt and moſt expeditious way to

LLANELLY,

a miſerable, dirty place, filled with miners and ſailors. From hence to

KIDWELY,

the road leads over the Penbree Hills; and from this elevation, the Scenery is viewed to great advantage.

The Caſtle of Kidwely, otherwiſe, *Cathweli,* was formerly, I imagine, of great extent, and is ſtill the moſt perfeſt we had hitherto met with in Wales. The extent of the apartments are diſtinguiſhable ; ſome of the ſtaircaſes acceſſible ; and the four round towers,

D keep,

keep, gateway, and yard, fpread an awful gloom around, whofe beauties time had juft fufficiently impaired, to heighten its grandeur and fublimity. Our Guide expatiated much on the Hiftory and Events of the Caftle, and told the ftory with as much agitation and intereft, as if it had happened yefterday.

The road to

CAERMARTHEN,

we found unpleafantly hilly, but occafional Vallies to our left enlivened our walk. Near Caermarthen we croffed a Bridge of free-ftone over the Towy. This River, running through the middle of this fhire, falls into the Britifh Sea at Caermarthen Bay, and is navigable for fmall veffels as far as the Bridge. Immediately over it, upon a hanging rock, ftand the remains of a once renowned Caftle. This Town, according to Giraldus's authority, was anciently a place of great ftrength, and fortified with brick walls, which are yet partly extant, near the river. This place, now confidered as the Capital of the county, was formerly the refidence of the Prince of South-Wales; and the Ancient Britons here held their Parliaments. The Chancery likewife, and Exchequer for South-Wales, were

were kept here, when this territory was firft erected into a Principality, by the crown of England. In the thirty-eighth year of Henry VIII. it was created a borough-town.

This place is famous for being the birth-place of Merlin, who is ftyled, by an ancient author, " the " fonne of a badde angell, or of an incubus fpirit, the " Britaine's great Apollo, whom Geoffrey ap Arthur " would ranke with the South-faying Seer, or rather " with the true Prophets themfelves; being none other " than a meere feducer, and phantafticall vizard." He flourifhed in the year 480.

At the Inn (Old Ivy-Bufh) Sir Richard Steel compofed his celebrated Play, called the *Confcious Lovers*.

From Caermarthen, we were recommended to go to

LAUGHARNE,

in order to fee the Caftle, but it by no means anfwered our expectation: little part of it now remains; and the neat gravel-walk, in the garden, but ill accords with the mutilated walls of an ancient ruin. From the garden walks, grand and extenfive Sea-profpects inte-

reft

reft the traveller.   About five miles from Laugharne, we paffed a fmall place, called

GREEN BRIDGE.

It derives its name from an excavation in the rock, through which a little rivulet runs for a mile and a half.   This cavity is completely concealed from the road, and impoffible to be difcovered, unlefs pointed out by fome neighbouring inhabitant.   Let me, however, advife all Tourifts to be cautious in their excurfions to this natural curiofity, as it is a place evidently calculated for plunder, ftratagems, and murder; and is now infefted by an unawed banditti of fmugglers, who have frequently practifed the barbarous fcheme of decoying veffels by falfe lights; and by whom we ourfelves were infulted.   Indeed, I would advife Travellers to alter their route from Swanfea, and purfue the ftraight road to Caermarthen, and fo to Tenby, by Narbeth.   By thefe means they efcape the unpleafant roads, (and almoft, indeed, inacceffible for carriages,) leading from Oyftermouth to Cheriton, and likewife from Llaugharne to Tenby.   But fhould the Tourift be led by an invincible curiofity to infpect the Ruins of Kidwely Caftle, it may eafily be accomplifhed, by purfuing the Turnpike-road to Kidwely, and from thence to Caermarthen :

marthen : in this laſt route you only omit viſiting the
Seat of Mr. Talbot, of Penrice ; though an object
highly worthy of inſpection.

At Saunders' Foot is a ſmall Bay, formed on one
ſide by a rock called the Monkſtone, and on the other
by the Caermarthenſhire coaſt. Near this place is
ſituate the Seat of Capt. Ackland ; and from thence to
Tenby, the dark lowering rocks roſe perpendicularly to
a conſiderable height, and then branched out into overhanging crags. It was now duſk ;—and at this tranſ-
forming hour, the bold promontories became ſhaded
with unreal glooms,—the projecting cliffs aſſumed a
more terrific aſpect,—and the wild, overhanging underwood,

" Wav'd to the gale in hoarſer murmurs."

TENBY,

is much reſorted to, during the ſummer months, for
bathing. It ſtands on a rock facing Caermarthen Bay :
the bold Promontory of the Monkſtone Head to the
North, and St. Catherine's Point, to the South, form
a fine Amphitheatre. The ſhore is well adapted for
bathing, the machines excellent, and a ſingular rock,

D 3   riſing rifing in the fea, clofe to the fhore, fhelters the bathing machines, even in the moft boifterous weather. On the South of Tenby, at the extremity of the fmall Ifland of St. Catherine's, attainable at low water, are the remains of a Roman Catholic Chapel. Entirely through this Ifland is a fingular perforation, which, without any difficulty, may be penetrated at the reflux of the tide. The Views from the South Sands are remarkably beautiful ; the character of the rocks is here awfully wild, craggy, and impending ; and the diftant fifhing-boats with their white fails, and the voices of the fifhermen, who conftantly frequent this coaft, borne at intervals on the air, are circumftances which animate the fcene : whilft the iflands of Caldy and St. Margaret's opportunely rife, to render the terrific ocean beautiful. The retrofpect is equally interefting ; the neat town of Tenby, with the mutilated walls of its Caftle, clofes this charming fcene.

The ancient walls of Tenby are ftill fufficiently perfect, to fhew its former ftrength and extent ; and the four round towers, ftanding on the extremity of the rock, point out the fituation of its Caftle. Near this is a ruinous building, fuppofed to be the remains of a Flemifh manufactory, probably woollen. On the North Sands is likewife another walk, equally beautiful, commanding the whole extent of Caermarthen Bay.

Bay. On the fummit of the rocks, over thefe fands, is the walk, called the *Croft :* on this eminence is fituaated the Hotel kept by Mr. Shaw; the accommodations are very good: the charges *per* week are eighteen fhillings board, finding your own tea, fugar, wine, and porter; fix fhillings for a bed-room, and at the fame rate a private parlour.

This place, from the vaft quantity of fifh caught near the coaft is called *Tenby-y-Pifcoid.*

If the Tourift has leifure and opportunity, many excurfions may be made during his ftay at Tenby. The firft, and moft important is, to Pembroke and Milford-Haven. The road affords many grand and extenfive Sea Views, with a faint profpect of Lundy Ifle. About four miles from Tenby, ftand the ruins of Mannorbeer Caftle, fuppofed to have been erected about the time of William Rufus. A little farther on, the ivy-mantled walls of Carew Caftle* burft upon us; and about three miles from Pembroke, the decayed and broken walls of Llanfeth, or Lantphey Caftle, attracted our notice, once the refidence of the Bifhops of St. David's, but now a monument of defolation. The three buildings of Swan-

* The Pedeftrian will not poffibly find time to examine the Ruins of Carew Caftle, in this day's route, but will find it more convenient to vifit it in his way from Tenby to Haverfordweft.

fea

fea Caftle, Lantphey Court, and King John's Hall,
St. David's, are very fimilar in their workmanfhip.
We now arrived at

PEMBROKE.

Mr. Wyndham has fo minutely delineated the Prefent
State of this Caftle, that I cannot do better than tranfcribe his account.

" The approach (fays this Author) to Pembroke
" from the River, fhews the Town and Caftle to the
" moft beautiful advantage. The Town is fituated
" upon the ridge of a long and narrow rock, gradually
" afcending to the higheft point, on which ftands the
" Caftle, at the brink of the precipice. If I may com-
" pare fmall things with great, it much refembles the
" fituation of Edinburgh.

" The Caftle is of Norman architecture, mixed with
" early Gothic. The principal tower, which is un-
" commonly high and perfect, has even its ftone vaulted
" roof remaining. The walls of this tower are four-
" teen feet in thicknefs, the diameter of the fpace
" within is twenty-five, and the heighth, from the
" ground to the crown of the dome, is feventy-five
                                        " feet ;

" feet; but vifible marks appear within, that its
" heighth was originally divided by four floors.

" Henry VII. was born in the prefent Caftle. The
" natural Cavern, called the Wogan, lies immediately
" under the Chapel, and opens with a wide mouth to-
" wards the river. A communication from the Cavern
" to the Caftle, was made by a ftair-cafe, on the outfide
" of the rock; the entrance was barricaded with a
" ftrong wall, partly remaining, thtough which there
" is now a large door-way opened to the fhore of the
" river. The Cavern appears nearly circular; its dia-
" meter is fifty-three feet; and its height is propor-
" tionable to the diameter.

" In the Civil War this Caftle was a garrifon for the
" Crown, and being befieged, made a gallant defence."

At Pembroke we hired a boat,* intending to fail
round the extenfive Haven of Milford; and, as we retired from the fhore, we took a retrofpect of the dilapidated walls of the Caftle, once the terror, and even in
ruins the pride of the fcene. It is moft advifable to make
this excurfion at high water, as it adds much to the
picturefque fcenery of the *tout enfemble.*

* The price for two oars, feven fhillings and fix-pence; and twelve
fhillings and fix-pence for four oars.

MILFORD

MILFORD HAVEN,

is juftly compared to " an immenfe lake; for the mouth
" not being at any diftance vifible, the whole Haven
" feems land-locked.   Though it is a mile and three
" quarters wide, it could not be defended againft an
" enemy, nor is there a fufficiency of timber in the
" neighbourhood.*   This Haven is formed by a great
" advance of the fea into the land, it being above ten
" miles from the Southermoft point at Nangle to Pem-
" broke, beyond which the tide comes up to and be-
" yond Carew Caftle.   It is capable of holding the
" whole navy of England, and the fame is faid of Cork
" Harbour.†   The fpring tides rife thirty-fix feet, the
" neap above twenty-fix.   Ships may be out of this
" Haven in an hour's time, and in eight or ten hours
" over at Ireland, or at the Land's End, and this with
" almoft any wind, by day or night."   Our reception
at the miferable place of

HUBBERSTON,

did not induce us to ftay longer than was fufficient to
recruit ourfelves.   We found the dirty Inn pre-occu-

* Wyndham, p. 72.   † Philofophical Survey of Ireland.

pied

pied by unfortunate Irish refugees: their situation was indeed melancholy;—driven from their country, their friends, and all, most dear to them!—And, wishing to forget their past sufferings, the following lines seem applicable to their situation:

> " Oh ! cou'd oblivion's friendly draught
> " Sooth all our sorrows to repose ;
> " Nor that intruder, restless thought,
> " Renew our agonizing woes!

> " Then all, unconscious of the past,
> " The present hour might calmly glide;
> " Keen retrospect no more be cast
> " O'er life's tempestuous, changeful tide:

> " Yet Heaven, to all its creatures kind,
> " With peace can gild the deepest gloom;
> " And, mid misfortune's wrecks, the mind
> " May sweet serenity assume."

Having refreshed ourselves, we walked to Milford, a small Village, opposite Hubberston: several comfortable houses are situated on the Hill, commanding a delightful View of the Haven. Being satisfied with our day's excursion, we again returned to our comfortable quarters at

TENBY,

TENBY,

which we left with regret a few days afterwards.——
We again purſued the Pembroke road ; and, about two
miles from Tenby, the neglected walls of Carew Caſtle
invited curioſity ;——and,

> Deep ſtruck with awe, we mark'd the dome o'erthrown,
> Where once the Beauty bloom'd, the Warrior ſhone :
> We ſaw the Caſtle's mouldering tow'rs decay'd,
> The looſe ſtone tott'ring o'er the trembling ſhade.

This Caſtle, I imagine, was intended more for a
noble reſidence, than a place of defence. The walls of
this building are very thick, and conſtructed with
ſtones, of a large ſize, ſtrongly cemented with mortar.
It is ſituated on a branch of Milford Haven, and conſiſts of a range of apartments built round a quadrangle,
with a circular tower at each corner. The South wall
is entirely demoliſhed ; but the North conſiſts of a
ſpacious hall, meaſuring one hundred and two feet
by twenty, ſuppoſed to have been built by Sir John
Perrot : above and under this hall, are noble apartments, and extenſive offices. This Caſtle appears to
have been erected at different times, if we may judge
from the architecture. Every ledge of the walls of the
towers,

towers, denoting the different ftories, were emboffed with vegetation, which feemed to grow from the folid ftone. Over the gate-way, at the Weft fide, are the arms of England, Duke of Lancafter, and Carew; and contiguous to this entrance, is another fpacious room, meafuring eighty feet by thirty.

In the Farm-yard, adjoining the Church, which has a lofty fquare Tower, is a dilapidated ftone-building, called the Parfonage.

Leaving Carew, we croffed a fmall Bridge over an arm of Milford Haven, and continued our route acrofs a barren and uninterefting heath; till, defcending to the Village of

CRESSELEY,

the luxuriant Plantation of Firs, belonging to Sir William Hamilton, attracted our attention. Small veffels conftantly frequent this quay, from whence a quantity of fmall coal is fhipped to different parts. From hence the road is extremely barren and unpicturefque; but, about three miles from

LAND-

LANDSHIPPING,

an arm of Milford Haven again burſt upon our ſight.——
Near it is ſituated the uninhabited houſe of Sir William
Owen. In croſſing the Ferry, Piƈton Caſtle, the property of Lord Milford, formed a prominent feature in
the gay ſcene ; and Slebitch, the Seat of Mr Philips,
ſtanding at the end of the Haven, contributes conſider-
ably to this piƈtureſque proſpeƈt.

The grounds of

PICTON,

through which we paſſed, about five miles in extent,
ſeemed to be well planned, and kept in excellent order.

This Caſtle has always been inhabited ; and having
eſcaped the fate of all other Caſtles in Wales, during
the civil wars, it retained, till very late, much of its
original external form. It is now occupied by Lord
Milford, and rendered a very comfortable ſummer reſidence. At the extremity of the Park, a good turnpike-
road ſoon conduƈted us to

HAVER-

HAVERFORD-WEST,

which is confidered as one of the largeft Towns in
South-Wales. It is very irregularly built, on the declivity of a hill, which is, in fome parts, fo very fteep,
that the ground-rooms frequently overlook the neighbouring roofs; yet there are fome good houfes. It is
confidered as a County of itfelf, and fends one Member
to Parliament. The Town was formerly fortified by a
ftrong wall, or rampart, on the Weftern fummit: the
fhell of a once-extenfive Caftle, is ftill remaining; this
is now converted into a goal.

The Parade, commanding a cheerful View of the
neighbouring Country, and the ruins of an ancient Abbey, extends for a confiderable way, by the fide of a hill.
At the extremity of this Walk, ftand the ruins of an
ancient Priory of Black Canons: the remains are now
very inconfiderable, but we eafily traced the Chapel,
over one end of which is an arch, ftill in good prefervation, and beautifully enwreathed with the rich drapery
of ivy.

Haverford is called by the Welch, *Hwlfordh*.* Having

* " The Caftle (fays an eminent Author) is faid to have been built by
" Gilbert Earl of Clare, who lived in the reign of King Stephen; and
" Camden

ing finifhed our furvey of Haverford, we ftarted early the next morning, purporting to breakfaft at

NEWGIN BRIDGE,

where we underftood we fhould meet with every thing comfortable; but, to our difappointment, we found a moft miferable, dirty pot-houfe, deftitute of even the common comforts of life. We were literally obliged to ftoop, in order to gain accefs to the Kitchen, which contained a fmall bed, and a few chairs; through this an elderly woman conducted us to what fhe diftinguifhed by the name of a Parlour: in this room the furniture confifted of two beds, a dirty table, and a few chairs. With difguft we left this miferable hovel, and contented ourfelves with a bafon of milk: we declined eating the bread, or rather oatmeal cake, which was of the coarfeft and hardeft nature. I here recollected Shenftone's complimentary lines on an Inn, but could not apply them on the prefent occafion:

" Camden reports, that Richard Earl of Clare made Richard Fitz-Tan-
" kred Governor thereof. It was one of thofe in the hands of the Fle-
" mings, when they firft came into Dyvet, or Pembrokefhire."

                                        " Whoe'er

"" Whoe'er has travell'd life's dull round,
  "" Where'er his stages may have been,
"" May sigh to think that he has found
  "" The warmest welcome at an Inn.""*

The road from Haverford to Newgin we found very uninteresting; and the shell of

ROACH CASTLE

did not detain us long. It stands on a rocky eminence, now completely in ruins, with only one tower remaining. "" Roach Castle (says Leland) in Rouseland, to "" the right of the road to St. David's, shews a round "" and some double out-works, visible at a great distance. "" It belonged to the Lords Ferrars and old Langeville, "" Knt. of Bucks.""

In descending the hill to Newgin, the dark lowering rocks, which form that fine Bay, called St. Bride's, exhibited a grand prospect. In the centre of this Bay is situated Newgin, bounded on the South by the Island of Skomar, and on the North by Ramsay. The fields adjacent to this place have been frequently inundated,

* These lines were frequently repeated by Dr. Johnson, whose partiality to Inns is well known.

E   by

by extraordinary overflowings of the fea: at the reflux of the tide, the fands admit of moft excellent walking.

The faunter from hence to the City of

ST. DAVIDS,

now properly deferving the name of a Village, was rather more captivating than our walk before breakfaft: it was occafionally enlivened by the profpect of the wide ocean, boundlefs to our view on one fide, whilft before us the fantaftic fhapes of the rocks off St. David's Head, exhibited Nature, in her moft awful and ftriking attitudes. Above the reft, Caern Thydy lifted its bold promontory, as if to give effect to the rude landfcape. About half way between Newgin and St. Davids, the beautiful little Village of Solva unexpectedly burft upon our view; ftudded with neat white-wafhed cottages, and enclofed on each fide with lofty rocks, which here form a picturefque and interefting chafm. Thefe rocks, indeed, I could almoft imagine, were torn afunder by fome convulfive rent of the earth. The Cathedral, and dilapidated ruins of the epifcopal Palace, are fituated at the bottom of a fteep hill, and fcarcely vifible in the town : thefe, and the prebendal houfes, were formerly enclofed by a ftrong ftone wall, with four gates, computed

puted at eleven hundred yards in circuit. David,* the national faint of Wales, with the confent of King Arthur, is faid to have removed the Metropolitan See from Cær Lleon to Menevia, which has ever fince been called *Ty Dewi*, by the Welch, and St. David, by the Englifh. What was the condition and extent of this town formerly, is difficult to fay, having been fo frequently deftroyed. At prefent it is a very fmall city, and has nothing to boaft, but its ruined palace, and old cathedral, dedicated to St. Andrew and St. David, which has often been demolifhed, but rebuilt, in its prefent form, by Bifhop Peter, according to Giraldus, in the reign of Henry II. or as Willis, 1110, in Rhos Vale, below the town. It is ftill efteemed a noble pile, confifting of two tranfepts, meafuring in length, from Eaft to Weft, three hundred feet, and the body, with the aifles, feventy-fix feet broad.

" Behind the choir is a moft beautiful chapel, with " a rich roof of carved ftone, built by Vaughan, in the

* " This celebrated perfon was uncle to King Arthur, and fon of a " Prince of Wales. After being feated in the fee of St. David fixty-five " years, and having built twelve monafteries; after having been exem- " plary in the piety of thofe days, this holy perfon died, at a moft ad- " vanced period of human life; having attained, as it is faid, to the age " of one hundred and forty-fix years. He was buried in the Cathedral " Church of St. David; and many years after canonized by Pope Califtus " the Second."—*Warrington's Hiftory of Wales*, vol. ii. p. 385.

" time

" time of Henry VIII. as a kind of prefbytery, between
" the choir and Lady chapel. In the laft, whofe roof,
" as well as thofe of the ailes of the choir and tran-
" fepts, have been down ever fince the civil war, are
" monuments for three bifhops, and in the nave, &c.
" four or five more. In the North wall of the choir
" is the fhrine of St. David, a kind of altar tomb, with
" a canopy of four pointed arches, and in front four
" quatrefoil holes, into which the votaries put their
" offerings, which were taken out by the Monks at two
" iron doors behind. In the choir are alfo the monu-
" ments of Owen Tudor, fecond hufband of Queen
" Catharine, Rhys ap Tudor,* Bifhops Jorwerth and
" Anfelm, in the 13th century, and Edmund Earl of
" Richmond, father of Henry VII. This laft monu-
" ment is faid to have prevented Henry VIII. from
" removing the fee to Caermarthen. Giraldus Cam-
" brenfis, who was Archdeacon of Brecon, canon of
" Hereford, and Rector of Chefterton, Oxford, was
" buried here 1213.† On the North fide of the church
" are fome walls of St. Mary's College, founded by
" Bifhop Houghton, and John of Gaunt, 1365, valued
" at 106l. *per annum.*"‡

* To whofe fon a MS. t. Elizabeth, quoted by Willis, p. 69, gives
Owen's monument.

† Tan. Bib. Brit.   ‡ Tan. 720.

It

It is much to be regretted, that so little regard has been paid to the internal appearance of this noble pile; the whole of it has lately been white-washed, which gives it too much the air of a modern building: the external part, I am sorry to add, has been equally neglected; and the chapels and monuments exposed to the wanton mischief of boys and idle people. The West front of the Cathedral has very lately been repaired by a Mr. Nash,* who has endeavoured, with bad success, to imitate the beautiful circular window remaining in the ruins of the Bishop's Palace. The stone, likewise, with which it is built, is of so soft a substance, that it even moulders with the touch of the finger; but possibly it may, by being exposed to the air, like the Bath stone, become more solid; and, when by time it shall have acquired a darker hue, may then better correspond with the original building.

The Bishop's Palace now stands a monument of desolation;—and as we walked over the loose fragments of stone, which are scattered through the immense area of the fabric, the images of former times rose to reflection,—when the spacious hall stood proudly in their original splendor; when the long ailes of the chapel were only responsive to the solemn, slow-breathed chaunt. In this Palace is a very long room, purposely

* This gentleman, I believe, is an inhabitant of Worcester.

E 3

erected

erected for the reception of King John: at the extremity of it is a circular window, of very elegant and curious workmanſhip.

Giraldus gives us a true deſcription of the counity round St. Davids, repreſenting it " as a ſtony, barren, " unimprovable territory, undecked with woods, undi- " vided by rivers, unadorned with meadows, expoſed " only to wind and ſtorms." Such, indeed, is the ſtate and ſituation of St. Davids; and, the environs having no hedges to divide the property of the farmers, the ſheep, and even the geeſe, are all tethered together.

The walk to St. David's Head, though barren, repreſents a view ſtriking and awful: ſublimity gives place to elegance: yet what is it to view?—a boundleſs waſte of ocean;—not a glimpſe of ſmiling nature, —not a patch of vegetation, to relieve the aching ſight, or vary the objects of admiration. The rocks on this ſhore, are ſhook into every poſſible ſhape of horror; and, in many parts, reſemble the convulſions of an earthquake, ſplintered, ſhivered, and amaſſed. On theſe rocks ſtood the famous rocking ſtone, or *Y mean ſigl*, which, " though twenty yoke of oxen could not " move it, might be ſhaken with the ſlighteſt touch." We underſtood it was thrown off its balance, by order of the farmer, to prevent the curious from trampling on his grounds. " A mile ſtrait Weſt from St. Da- " vid's,

" vid's, betwixt Portclais and Porthmaur,"* is the shell of Capel Stinen, St. Stinan's, or St. Justinian's Chapel.

From this spot is an extensive View of Whitsand Bay, called by the Welsh *Porth Maur*, or the Great Bay; in which stand the six Rocks, called *The Bishop and his Clerks.* Half a league from hence is

RAMSEY ISLE,

half a mile long, and three quarters broad, and divided into two considerable farms. The whole island is well stocked with rabbits; and, during the Spring, the Razorbill, Puffin, and Harry Birds, resort here in flocks.

Our walk, from St. Davids to

FISHGUARD,

afforded us little room for observation; the eye, however, kept in view a wide range of the unbounded ocean, till, dim with exertion, it by degrees reposed on the dark lowering rocks, which, disregarding the angry roar of the waves, seemed to project their broad sides, to augment the idle tumult. Quittting the turnpike

* Lland, vol. v. p. 25.

road,

road, in fearch of the place where the French effected
their landing in 1797, we paffed a neat houfe, called
Caergwent, belonging to Mrs. Harris.   The kind attentions of a farmer, in the neighbourhood of this memorable fpot, claim our warmeft acknowledgments.
Having finifhed a moft comfortable meal at Mr. Mortimer's houfe, (which, during the confufion was confidered the head-quarters of the French, commanded by
General Tate) he explained every minutiæ refpecting
this circumftance; and very obligingly pointed out the
fituation of their camp, and related many entertaining
and interefting anecdotes.   Deeply impreffed with gratitude towards Mr. M. for his civilities, we foon arrived
at Goodric Sands.   This fpot was very judicioufly felected by Lord Cawdor, as a proper place for the French
to lay down their arms; for, had they refifted, a can-
nonade of grape-fhot, from a neighbouring fortrefs,
would have inftantly played upon them.   Fifhguard
ftands on a fteep rock, with a convenient harbour,
formed by the river Gwain; though its fituation and
Bay are interefting, it is by no means a defirable place
to remain long at.

Several Druidical Monuments* engaged our attention, as we drew near

* For a defcription of thefe Monuments, fee Wyndham.

NEW-

NEWPORT,

called by Giraldus Llanhever, or The Town on the River Nevern. The fragments of the Caftle are too infignificant to invite the curiofity of the paffing traveller: it was demolifhed by Llewellyn, Prince of South-Wales, when poffeffed by the Flemings.

The country beyond Newport prefented a more pleafing countenance: wood, water, hill, and vale, all unite, even to induce the plodding citizen to paufe, and wifh to fpend the evening of his days in the vicinity of its enchantment. In this interefting fituation, we found the Village of Velindre:—we here particularly obferved the flaty quality of the hills, and could not avoid condemning the folly of the inhabitants of Velindre, in building their cottages of mud, and fparingly covering them with ftraw, when Nature herfelf feemed to place comforts, if not luxuries, before their view. But, perhaps, thefe reproaches were ill-grounded: for, thus veiled in obfcurity, they were happy, as they knew not enough of the world ferioufly to regret the want of thefe conveniencies: their fituation, indeed, feemed to verify the philofophical fentiment of Gray:

> " Since ignorance is blifs,
> " 'Tis folly to be wife."

For

For though they fuffer the extremes of filth and penury, yet they enjoy the two ineftimable bleffings, health and felicity.

The broken towers of

KILGERRAN CASTLE,

foon attracted our notice. The relicks of this ruin ftand on a point of rock, impending over the river Tyvi, whofe beauty time had only impaired, to heighten its grandeur. Two imperfect circular towers, and the fragments of a wall, now only remain. The river Tyvi, I imagine, abounds with fifh, as we obferved at every door, in the village of Kilgerran, a coracle.* The conftruction of this little water conveyance is remarkably fimple, and intended folely for the ufe of fifhing: a thick fkin, or coarfe pitched canvas, is ftretched over *wicker-work*. This fingular fifhing-boat only conveys one man, who manages it with the greateft adroitnefs imaginable; the right hand being employed in ufing the paddle, the left in conducting the net, and the teeth in holding the line. Two coracles generally co-operate, to affift each other in fifhing: they ufually

---

* It receives its name from *coria*, a hide, or fkin.

meafure

meafure about five feet long, and four broad, and rounded at the corners; and, after the labours of the day, are conveyed, on the back, to the little cot of the fifherman, which is looked upon as a neceffary appendage to the cottage door.

Defcription can fcarcely fuggeft the full magnificence and beauty of the faunter from hence to Cardigan: the valley, about two miles in extent, feemed to poffefs all that Nature inherits; floping hills, two hundred feet high, covered with wood, from the water's edge, to their higheft fummit, and at the moft acceptable diftances, and truly happy fituations, interrupted by a bold, naked, and projecting rock: whilft the broad and tranflucid ftream of the Tyvi reflects, as in a mirror, the blacknefs of the impending fhades. The retrofpect commands the romantic ruins of Kilgarran Caftle, whofe mutilated walls clofe this delicious landfcape. The whole valley bears a ftrong refemblance to the fituation of the celebrated Piercefield. As this fpot is entirely loft, by keeping the turnpike road, it is advifable for travellers, in general, to hire a boat from Cardigan to Kilgarran: this, our humble and lefs-encumbered mode of travelling rendered unneceffary.

At Llechryd, not far from Kilgerran, extenfive Tin-works are carried on by Sir Benjamin Hamet.
Having

Having already examined works of this nature at Neath, we preferred the romantic vale of Kilgerran; as to accomplish both, would have occupied too much time.

We entered the town of

CARDIGAN,

over a handfome ftone-bridge, built over the Tyvi, which is here of confiderable width. In front of this ftands, on a fteep eminence, the Caftle, confifting chiefly of its outer walls, which prove it to have been once a confiderable building. This place, confidered the principal town of the county, is called by the Britons *Abertuvi*; which name it receives from ftanding near the *Mouth of the River Tyvi*. It was fortified, together with the Caftle, by Gilbert, fon of Richard Clare, and demolifhed by Rhees ap Gryffith.

The town is large, and regular; its chief trade confifting in lead, exported to Ireland. The Church is large, and well-built, with a handfome tower. The new gaol, finifhed in 1797, is conveniently fituated, and appears to be a well-planned building.

One

One mile Weft from Cardigan is

ST. DOGMAEL's ABBEY,

called, by Leland,* a " Priory of Bonhommes." The
Monafticon places this houfe amongft the Benedictines;
but it was that ftrict and reformed fort of Benedictines,
called the order of *Tiron*, founded by *Martin of Tours*,
who conquered the country of Cemmeis, about the time
of King William the Conqueror. Part of the ruins
is now converted into a chapel, for the convenience of
the vicinity.

At the fecond mile ftone, in our road from Cardigan,
to the village of

LLANARTH,

we halted a fhort time, to take a retrofpect of the
country we had paffed. From this fpot, the Town and
Caftle of Cardigan, ftanding on an eminence, in the
centre of a broad valley, and encircled with hills, beautifully introduced themfelves to our view. From
hence to

* Itin. vol. v. p. 124

ABE-

ABERAERON,

grand Sea profpects continued to enliven our route;—— whilft the faint and ftill fainter hues of the coaft of Ireland appeared juft vifibly fkirting the diftant horizon.

Aberaeron is fituated in a vale, near the conflux of the river Aeron with the fea : from whence it receives its name; *Aber* fignifying the *mouth* of any thing.

The entrenchment, mentioned by Sael, in his *Collection of Tours*, about a mile from Aberaeron, is now almoft wafhed away, by the daily encroachments of the fea.   We lamented, that the Druidical fepulchral monuments, mentioned by the fame Author, were inadvertently paffed unnoticed by us.

In this day's journey, we ftill continued to indulge the fublime emotions, which an unconfined view of the ocean always infpires; a ferene day, with partial gleams of funfhine, gave magical effects to the fcenery; and the fea was enlivened with many a veffel, whofe gay ftreamers, glittering to the fun-beams, prefented to the eye a conftant moving fcene, and rendered the terrific ocean beautiful.   Before us, the towering mountains of Merionethfhire

rionethſhire glittered in all thoſe colours of beauty, which conſtitute the ſublime; and we appeared only to climb one hill, to view ſtill others riſing in endleſs perſpective: over the whole was diffuſed the rich glow of even; and the diſtant mountains were variegated by the parting tinge of lingering day. A neat Church, backed by romantic hills, animated the village of Llanryſted. Three miles from

ABERYSTWITH,

we pauſed at Llanryan Bridge, to admire the rich banks riſing on each ſide of the river Yſtwith, over which this bridge is thrown; it is built in the ſtyle of the celebrated Pont y Prydd, in the vale of Glamorganſhire. We entered the town of Aberyſtwith, over a temporary wooden bridge.* In the year 1796, a ſtone bridge experienced the ſame fate with many others in Wales, occaſioned by a ſudden thaw: Mr. Edwards, from Dolgelly is now engaged in erecting another, by contract, conſiſting of ſix arches.

Aberyſtwith, partaking much of the dirt of ſeaports in general, is ſituated at the termination of

* Over the river Rhydal.

the

the vale of Rhydol, in the Bay of Cardigan, and open to St. George's Channel. The environs are ftony and rugged; the coaft affords indifferent bathing, being much expofed; and the fhore rough and unpleafant. In fine, it is, in almoft all refpects, the reverfe of Tenby, except it has the advantage in the number of houfes, and, confequently, more company. At the extremity of the town, upon an eminence, ftand the ruins of an ancient caftle, of which little now remains but a folitary tower, overlooking a wide expanfe of fea. It was rendered famous, by being, at one time, the refidence of the great Cadwalader, and in all the Welch wars confidered as a fortrefs of great ftrength: it was built by Gilbert Strongbow, 1107, and rebuilt by Edward I. in 1277, a few years before his complete conqueft of Wales. The ruin of the caftle now affords a pleafant walk.

But what formerly rendered this town more confiderable, were the rich Lead Mines in its vicinity. Thefe mines are faid to have yielded near a hundred ounces of filver from a ton of lead, and to have produced a profit of two thoufand pounds a month. Sir Hugh Middleton here made the vaft fortune, which he afterwards expended on the New River, conftructed for the purpofe of fupplying the Northern fide of London with water. But Thomas Bufhell raifed thefe mines to their

greateft

greateſt height: an indenture was granted to him by Charles I. for the coining of ſilver pieces, to be ſtamped with oſtrich feathers, on both ſides, for the benefit of paying his workmen. This gentleman was afterwards appointed Governor of Lundy Iſle. The moſt conſiderable lead mine was that of Bwlch-yr-Eſkir-his, diſcovered in 1690. The ore was here ſo near the ſurface, that the moſs and graſs in ſome places juſt covered it.

Cloſe to the ſcite of the old Caſtle, Mr. Uvedale Price, of Foxley in Herefordſhire, has erected a fantaſtic houſe, in the caſtellated form, intended merely as a ſummer reſidence. Mr. Naſh, of Caermarthen, was the architect: it conſiſts of three octagon towers, with a balcony towards the ſea. The rooms are well contrived, and elegantly furniſhed: the windows command an unlimited View of St. George's Channel ; and the dilapidated fragments of the Caſtle, are from hence viewed to great advantage.

We determined to purſue the Banks of the meandering Rhyddol, in preference to the turnpike road, in our way to Havod.

This valley comprehends every thing that conſtitutes the beautiful : it is encloſed by high mountains oh

F each

each fide, vegetating to their fummits; indeed, all the
tints of verdure, and diverfity of foliage, here introduce
themfelves in one view; the Rhyddol ftruggling with the
huge maffes of rock,—its never-ceafing, tumultuous motion,—its fparkling foam;—in fine, every thing that can
be imagined, by the moft enthufiaftic admirer of nature
is blended in this fhort excurfion :—

> ————————————" *is not this vale*
> " More free from peril than the envious courts?
> " Here feel we but the penalty of Adam,
> " The feafon's difference, as the icy fang
> " And churlifh chiding of the Winter's wind."
>
> SHAKSPEARE.

To the inquifitive pedeftrian, for this vale is inacceffible for carriages, the old Church of Llanbadem
Vawr, which fignifies *The Church of Great Paternus*, a
native of Bretagne, is particularly interefting; who, as
the writer of his Life expreffes it, " by feeding go-
" verned, and by governing fed the Church of Cere-
" tica." To his memory this Church, and formerly
an Epifcopal See was founded: but the Bifhopric, as
Roger Hovedan writes, " early declined, becaufe the
" parifhioners flew their paftor.*

* The additions to Camden 1695, fuppofe this, Bifhop Idnert,

As

As we drew near the

DEVIL's BRIDGE,

a long chain of mountains excited our admiration, encircled half way down with a thick mift, fimilar in appearance to a girdle: this circumftance feems to juftify
the bold imagery, and beautiful defcription of a mountain given by the Poet:

"" As fome tall cliff that lifts its awful form
"" Swells from the vale, and midway leaves the ftorm;
"" Though round its breaft the rolling clouds are fpread,
"" Eternal funfhine fettles on its head."—GOLDSMITH.

The comfortable Inn, fituated near this romantic fpot,
ftands in front of the river Rhyddol, and commanding
the moft picturefque view fancy can paint, is built by
the refpectable and truly hofpitable owner of Havod.

This celebrated Bridge, fo much the object of curiofity and admiration, is fo completely environed with
trees, that many travellers, not intent upon deep inveftigation, or in purfuit of nature's landfcapes, may pafs
over it, without the leaft fufpicion of the dreadful aper-
ture, or the ancient ftructure, that conveys them over

F 2   the

the gulf. On the Eastern side we descended a preci-
pitous, and treacherous bank, consisting of slate rock,
or *laminac*, I should imagine, near a hundred feet: this
is the computed measurement; but the eye, confused by
the awfulness of the scene, loses its faculty of judging.
From this spot, the vast chine, or chasm, over which
the bridge is thrown, is seen to great advantage: the
whole of this fissure was probably occasioned by some
convulsion of nature, as each indenture seems to correspond with the opposite protuberance. Under the
bridge, the river Mynach, in its confined course, meeting with obstructions of massy rock, and fragments of
prodigious size, rushes through the chasm with irresistible violence.

This bridge is called in Welsh *Pont-ar-Fynach*, or
Mynach Bridge: it consists of two arches, one thrown
over the other. The foundation of the under one is
of great antiquity, and vulgarly attributed to the inven-
tion of the Devil: it is supposed to have been erected
as far back as the year 1087, in the reign of William II., by the Monks of Strata Florida Abbey, the
ruins of which are still visible, about ten miles from
hence. Gerald mentions his passing over it, when he
accompanied Baldwin, Archbishop of Cambray, at the
time of the crusades, in the year 1188, and in the reign
of Richard I. The original arch being suspected to be

in

in a ruinous condition, the prefent bridge was built over it, at the expence of the county, in the year 1753.——The width of the chafm is eftimated at about thirty feet.

Our Ciceroni firft conducted us to a fall on the river Rhyddol, unobferved in Walker's *Defcription of the Devil's Bridge*, and unnoticed by Warner. The character of this fall is remarkably fingular : a huge fragment of rock, projecting over the river for a confiderable way, precipitates the water in a fingular, and almoft inexpreffible direction ; the rocks are occafionally variegated by the dark foliage of underwood, and fometimes barren, rugged, and impending.

Defcription cannot fuggeft the full magnificence of the profpect which fpread before us, on our arrival at the grand fall of the Mynach ; for though it may paint the grandeur of the elegance of outline, yet it cannot equal the archetypes in nature, or draw the minute features, that reward the actual obferver, at every new choice of his pofition : reviewing this thundering cataract, in the leifure of recollection, thefe nervous lines of Thomfon feem to defcribe much of the fcene :

" Smooth to the fhelving brink a copious flood
" Rolls fair and placid, where collected all
" In one impetuous torrent, down the fteep
" It thundering fhoots, and fhakes the country round.

" At

" At firſt an azure ſheet, it ruſhes broad ;
" Then whitening by degrees, as prone it falls,
" And from the loud-reſounding rocks below
" Daſh'd in a cloud of foam, it ſends aloft
" A hoary miſt, and forms a ceaſeleſs ſhower.
" Nor can the tortur'd wave here find repoſe :
" But raging ſtill amid the ſhaggy rocks,
" Now flaſhes o'er the ſcatter'd fragments, now
" Aſlant the hollow channel rapid darts ;
" And falling faſt from gradual ſlope to ſlope,
" With wild infraƈted courſe, and leſſen'd roar,
" It gains a ſafer bed, and ſteals, at laſt,
" Along the mazes of the quiet vale."

The following Table, taken from Walker's *Deſcrip-tion of the Devil's Bridge*, gives the exaƈt height from the top of the bridge, to the water underneath, and the different falls from thence, till the Mynach delivers it-ſelf into the Rhyddol below :

FALLS, &c.

	Feet.
From the Bridge to the Water -	114
Firſt Fall - - -	18
Second ditto - - -	60
Third ditto - - -	20
Grand Cataraƈt - -	110
From the Bridge to the Rhyddol -	322

The

The rocks on each fide of the fall rife perpendicularly to the height of eight hundred feet, and finely clothed with the richeft vegetation, to its higheft fummit.

Near the bafon of the firft fall from the bridge we entered a dark cavern, formerly inhabited by a fet of robbers, two brothers and a fifter, called *Plant Mat*, or *Plant Fat*, fignifying Matthew's Children. Tradition reports, that they committed various depredations in the neighbourhood, and lived concealed in this " *fpecus* " *horrendum*" for many years, from the keen refearch of " day's garifh eye." The entrance juft admits fufficient light to make " darknefs vifible."

With regret we left this romantic fpot; where, if Retirement ever had " local habitation," this was her " place of deareft refidence." " One excurfion (fays " Mr. Cumberland) to this place will not fuffice com- " mon obfervers; nor indeed many, to the lovers of " the grand fports of Nature." The Mynach (in " another place he defcribes) coming down from be- " neath the Devil's Bridge, has no equal for height or " beauty that I know of; for although a ftreamlet, to " the famous fall of Narni in Italy, yet it rivals it in " height, and furpaffes it in elegance.

F 4

" After

" After paſſing deep below the bridge, as through a
" narrow firth, with noiſes loud and ruinous, into a
" confined chaſm, the fleet waters pour headlong and
" impetuous, and leaping from rock to rock, with fury,
" literally laſh the mountain's ſides; ſometimes almoſt
" imbower'd among deep groves, and flaſhing, at laſt,
" into a fan-like form, they fall rattling among the
" looſe ſtones of the Devil's Hole—where, to all ap-
" pearance, it ſhoots into a gulf beneath, and ſilently
" ſteals away: for ſo much is carried off in ſpray,
" during the inceſſant repercuſſions it experiences, in
" this long tortuous ſhoot, that, in all probability, not
" half the water arrives at the bottom of its profound
" and ſullen grave."

Four miles from hence, on the Llandiloe's road, is
ſituated

HAVOD,

the celebrated Seat of Mr. Johnes.   The former part
of the road is barren and unintereſting : but on our firſt
entrance into the grounds, all our paſt complaints were
loſt in expreſſions of admiration.   The manſion is a
very elegant piece of architecture built of Portland
ſtone, and the plan entirely novel, being a mixture of

the

the Moorish and Gothic, with turrets and painted windows. The whole of it indeed does great credit to the architect, Mr. Baldwyn of Bath. It is situated near the banks of the river Ystwith, and beautifully environed by lofty hills, clothed with oak. The interior of the house corresponds in elegance with the exterior. From the hall we were conducted through a suite of elegant apartments, very judiciously fitted up with paintings, statues, and antiques; but the Library more particularly engaged our notice, containing a choice and valuable collection of books; this octagonal room is built in the form of a dome, with a gallery round it, supported by a colonade of variegated marble pillars, of the ancient Doric order, with a circular window at top, for the admission of light. We entered through a handsome door, inlaid with a large reflecting mirror; immediately opposite is another door, of transparent plateglass, leading to the Conservatory, three hundred feet in length, and containing a number of curious, and rare exotics, with a walk down the centre of the building. In fine, the effect of the *tout ensemble* can better be imagined than described. Amongst the other things worthy of admiration, a handsome statue, in the Library, of Thetis dipping Anchises in the river Styx more particularly detains attention. We next passed through the Billiard-room, and were conducted to the top of the stair-case, to admire two elegant paintings,

the

the fubjects taken from Capt. Cook's Voyages: the
painter is unknown. Many of the rooms are beautifully furnifhed with rich Gobelin tapeftry.

To give my readers a juft conception of the beauties
of Havod, I fhall beg leave to borrow the elegant defcription of it, drawn by the mafterly pen of Mr. Cumberland.

"Havod," fays Mr. Cumberland, "is a place in it-
"felf fo pre-eminently beautiful, that it highly merits
"a particular defcription. It ftands furrounded with
"fo many noble fcenes, diverfified with elegance, as
"well as with grandeur; the country on the approach
"to it is fo very wild and uncommon, and the place
"itfelf is now fo embellifhed by art, that it will be dif-
"ficult, I believe, to point out a fpot that can be put
"in competition with it, confidered either as the object
"of the Painter's eye, the Poet's mind, or as a defirable
"refidence for thofe who, admirers of the beautiful
"wildnefs of nature, love alfo to inhale the pure air
"of afpiring mountains, and enjoy that *fanto pacè* (as
"the Italians expreffively term it,) which arifes from
"folitudes made focial by a family circle.

"From the portico, it commands a woody, narrow,
"winding vale; the undulating forms of whofe afcend-
"ing,

" ing, fhaggy fides, are richly cloathed with various
" foliage, broken with filver water-falls, and crowned
" with climbing fheep-walks, reaching to the clouds.

" Neither are the luxuries of life abfent; for, on the
" margin of the Yftwith, where it flows broadeft
" through this delicious vale, we fee hot-houfes, and a
" confervatory; beneath the rocks, a bath; amid the
" receffes of the woods, a flower-garden; and within
" the building, whofe decorations, though rich, are
" pure and fimple, we find a mafs of rare and valuable
" literature, whofe pages here feem doubly precious,
" where meditation finds fcope to range unmolefted.

" In a word, fo many are the delights afforded by
" the fcenery of this place, and its vicinity, to a mind
" imbued with any tafte, that the impreffion on mine
" was increafed, after an interval of ten years from the
" firft vifit, employed chiefly in travelling among the
" Alps, the Appenines, the Sabine Hills, and the Ty-
" rollefe; along the fhores of the Adriatic, over the
" Glaciers of Switzerland, and up the Rhine; where,
" though in fearch of beauty, I never, I feel, faw any
" thing fo fine—never fo many pictures concentred in
" one fpot; fo that, warned by the renewal of my ac-
" quaintance with them, I am irrefiftibly urged to at-
" tempt

" tempt a defcription of the hitherto almoft virgin-
" haunts of thefe obfcure mountains.

" Wales, and its borders, both North and South,
" abound, at intervals, with fine things: Piercefield
" has grounds of great magnificence, and wonderfully
" picturefque beauty. Downton Caftle has a delicious
" woody vale, moft taftefully managed; Llangollen is
" brilliant; the banks of the Conway favagely grand;
" Barmouth romantically rural; the great Piftill Rhay-
" ader is horribly wild; Rhayader Wennol, gay, and
" glorioufly irregular—each of which merits a ftudied
" defcription.

" But, at Havod, and its neighbourhood, I find the
" effects of all in one circle; united with this pecu-
" liarity, that the deep dingles, and mighty woody
" flopes, which from a different fource, conduct the
" Rhyddol's never-failing waters from Plynlimmon,
" and the Fynach, are of an unique character, as
" mountainous forefts, accompanying gigantic fize
" with graceful forms; and, taken altogether, I fee
" the ' fweeteft interchange of hill and valley, rivers,
" woods, and plains, and falls, with forefts crowned,
" rocks, dens, and caves;' infomuch, that it requires
" little enthufiafm there to feel forcibly with Milton,
" with

                                            " All

" All things that be, fend up from earth's great altar
" Silent praife!"

" There are four fine walks from the houfe, chiefly
" through ways artificially made by the proprietor;
" all dry, kept clean, and compofed of materials found
" on the fpot; which is chiefly a courfe ftone, of a
" greyifh caft, friable in many places, and like flate,
" but oftener confifting of immenfe maffes, that coft
" the miner, in making fome part of thefe walks, ex-
" ceffive labour; for there are places, where it was
" neceffary to perforate the rock many yards, in order
" to pafs a promontory, that, jutting acrofs the way,
" denied further accefs; and to go round which, you
" muft have taken a great tour, and made a fatiguing
" defcent. As it is, the walks are fo conducted, that
" few are fteep; the tranfitions eafy, the returns com-
" modious, and the branches diftinct. Neither are
" they too many, for much is left for future projectors;
" and if a man be ftout enough to range the under-
" woods, and faftidious enough to reject all trodden
" paths, he may, almoft every where, ftroll from the
" ftudied line, till he be glad to regain the friendly con-
" duct of the well-known way.

" Yet one muft be nice, not to be content at firft
" to vifit the beft points of view by the general rou-
" tine;

" tine; for all that is here done, has been to remove
" obstructions, reduce the materials, and conceal the
" art; and we are no where presented with attempts
" to force these untamed streams, or indeed to invent
" any thing, where nature, the great mistress, has left
" all art behind."

We now for many miles passed a barren, dreary
country, completely encircled with hills, and we only
climbed one, to observe still others rising in the distant
perspective: not even a house or tree appeared to inter-
rupt the awfulness of the mountains, which after the
copious fall of rain in the night, teemed with innumerable cataracts.   According to our directions, we enquired at the foot of Plinlimmon for Rhees Morgan, as
a proper man to be our conductor over the heights of the
" fruitful father of rivers."   This man being absent,
the whole family appeared thunderstruck at our appearance, and run with all haste imaginable into their
miserable cot, or which might rather be dignified with
the appellation of a pig-stye; as that *filthy animal* seemed
to claim, with the wretched family, an equal right to
a share of the hovel.   One apartment served for the inhabitants of every description, with only one small hole
to admit the light; the entrance unprotected by a door,
but with a blanket as a substitute, was exposed to the
pitiless blast of the winter's storm.   Reviewing this de-
spicable

fpicable hovel, I recalled to my mind a very juft obfervation of Goldfmith's, " That one half of the world
" are ignorant how the other half lives."

 " Ah ! little think the gay licentious proud
 " Whom pleafure, power, and affluence furround ;
 " They, who their thoughtlefs hours in giddy mirth,
 " And wanton, often cruel, riot wafte;
 " Ah ! little think they, while they dance along,

 ———————" how many drink the cup
 " Of baleful grief, or eat the bitter bread
 " Of mifery. Sore pierc'd by wintry winds,
 " How many fhrink into the fordid hut
 " Of cheerlefs poverty."———THOMPSON.

With fome difficulty we prevailed on the female part
of the family to give us proper directions to the fource
of the meandering Wye,* and rapid Severn. The
latter they only underftood by the name of *Halfren*, its
original Britifh name; it is likewife called in Latin
Sabrina. From the top of Plinlimmon we, for the
firft time, difcovered the fhaggy fummit of Cader Idris,
and the fpiral head of Snowdon. There is nothing
particularly engaging in the character of this mountain, except to its giving rife to no lefs than fix or eight

* Called in Latin *Vaga*.

rivers,

rivers, and on this account has frequently been celebrated by the Poet. Though its summit commands a circle of many miles diameter, yet the prospect by no means answered our expectations. We descended into a swampy bottom, which afforded us unpleasant walking for two or three miles, when a most delightful and well-cultivated valley unexpectedly enlivened our spirits. The sun was making

> ——————————" a golden set,
> " And by the bright track of his fiery car
> " Gave signal of a goodly day to-morrow,"

just as we entered this interesting vale : the hay-makers, in the coolness of the evening, were returning to their homes,

> " Each by the lass he loved."

In short, the whole valley breathed delicious fragrance: add to this, innumerable cataracts rushed from the mountain's summits, occasioned by the late copious rains.

From hence a good turnpike-road soon conducted us to the romantic town of

MACHYNLLETH,

considered as the center of the woollen manufactory in this

this part of the country, principally of the *ftrong cloth*, or *high country cloth*.* The fituation of Machynlleth, (or as it is pronounced by the Welch, *Mahunthleth*) is extremely romantic, ftupendous mountains forming a natural rampart round the town. We here vifited the neglected Manfion, where Owen Glendwr affembled the States of the Principality, in 1402, and accepted from their hands the crown of Wales. Part of the houfe is now allotted for the purpofe of a ftable, the remainder is turned into a butcher's fhop :—

"*Sic tranfit gloria mundi !*"

In fine, the only evident remains of its ever having been celebrated in the annals of hiftory, is a fpacious door way. The town itfelf, in many parts, bears the appearance of antiquity; the ftreets are confiderably wider than Welch towns in general, and the market-place is well built.

As we entered Machynlleth, being the firft town in North Wales, we were in a manner inftinctively induced to reflect on the various incidents that had befallen us from our firft fallying forth on our pedeftrian excurfion. We took a retrofpect on all our little trou-

* See an excellent account of the woollen manufactory in the feventh chapter of Aikin's Tour through North Wales.

G   bles,

bles, with equally as much delight, as the failor, who,
by the bleffing of Providence, has efcaped the moft
imminent dangers: all our paft imaginary dangers
(for imaginary evils are frequently worfe than real
ones) were overbalanced with reflections on the many
hours of pleafure that were flown unheeded by: thefe
reflections brought to my recollection fome interefting
lines in Bowles's Sonnets, which I involuntarily ex-
claimed aloud,

> " Fair fcenes ye lend a pleafure long unknown
> " To him who paffes weary on his way ;
> " The farewell tear, which now he turns to pay
> " Shall thank you ; and whene'er of pleafures flown,
> " His heart fome long-loft image would renew,
> " Delightful haunts ! he will remember you."

The fublimity of the walk from hence to *Talylyn*,
literally " beggars description." Having croffed a
bridge of eight arches, thrown over the river Do-
vey, high mountains clofed us on every fide, fhook
into every poffible form of horror; huge maffes of
rock hung over the road, and it feemed neceffary to
remember their firm bafis, to foften the terror they infpired ; whilft other mifhapen fragments lie fcattered
at the fide of the road. The tranfparent Dyflas, whofe
clear furface reflected the tremulous picture in all its
colours, forms one continued cataract for five or fix
miles,

miles, overflowing with the innumerable tributary torrents, which hurry themselves down from the higheft
fummit of the furrounding rocks; whilft to give effect
to the whole profpect, the fhaggy head of Cader Idris
towers the majeftic fentinel of the fcene, whofe "cloud
"cap'd" fummit the eye aches in furveying. To our
great difappointment, the weather prevented our afcending this celebrated mountain giant. Cader Idris is
efteemed, in height, the fecond mountain in all Wales,
rifing two thoufand eight hundred and fifty feet above
the green of Dolgelly.*

If the weather proves favorable to afcend Cader
Idris, travellers may be very comfortably accommodated with beds at

TALYLYN;

a fmall village, fituated at the foot of the mountain;
and where they will likewife meet with a conductor, in
every refpect fuited for this Alpine excurfion. Mr.
Jones, the landlord of the Blue Lion, ufed all his influence to perfuade us, by largely expatiating on the
comforts of his accommodations, to detain us till the

* See Pennant's Snowdonia, p. 89, and likewife Wilfon's excellent
View of Cader Idris.

weather

weather wore a more favorable afpect, but knowing the
uncertainty of his conjectures, we determined to make
Barmouth our head quarters.   Quitting therefore oar
officioufly polite landlord, we foon arrived at the Pool
of Three Grains, which, though of inferior fize, yet is
generally credited to be unfathomable ; it abounds in
fifh, and derives its name from three immenfe ftones,
or rather fragments of rock near it, which the common
people confidently affert, and believe, the giant Idris
took out of his fhoes as he paffed this pool.

Having afcended feveral hills, a quick defcent of
three or four miles, foon brought us to

DOLGELLY;

furrounded with " a tempeftuous fea of mountains,"
and watered by the rapid current of the river Avon-
vawr, over which is thrown a large and handfome
ftone bridge, at the entrance of the town.

In the neighbourhood of this romantic fpot, and
indeed in many parts of Merionethfhire, the manufac-
ture of ftrong cloth has long been carried on.*

We

---

* Mr. Pennant, in his Snowdonia, p. 397, publifhed in 1781, " men-
" tions, that there are brought annually to Salop 700,000 yards of web ;
" and

We were reluctantly neceffitated to leave this interefting town of Dolgelly, much fooner than we wifhed, had we obeyed our own inclinations. No one can picture to themfelves a more picturefque fituation than that of Dolgelly:—an enclofed vale, encircled with the craggy and fubject mountains of Cader Idris, forming an amphitheatre,—watered by the Alpine torrent of the Maw,—and richly clothed with wood. But neceffity has no law ; the beft Inn was pre-occupied, and no comfortable accommodations could be found, and though drenched with rain, we were compelled to quicken our pace to the well-known bathing place of

BARMOUTH.

It is advifeable for all travellers, pedeftrians not excepted, to leave Dolgelly at high water, as without that, the fcenery lofes much of its beauty ; if convenient, it is certainly preferable to hire a boat, at the Stoves ; the charge is three fhillings and fixpence ; by this you will fave a walk of eight miles, and both from

"" and to Welch Pool, annually, between 7 and 800,000 yards of flannel ;
"" but he does not ftate the particulars whence he reduces his general
"" eftimate." I have quoted this paffage from Aikin's excellent chapter
(vii.) on the Woollen Manufactures of North Wales, not having in my
poffeffion Mr. P.'s Snowdonia.

G 3   your

your fituation, and from being more at your eafe, will better admit of your obferving the furrounding fcenery, with which you cannot fail to be highly gratified.

This fhort excurfion of eight miles, is truly grand, awful, and fublime; and though many parts of this ftriking valley are richly cultivated, yet, by the fide of the road, enormous mountains, formed into the moft capricious fhapes, fhoot into the clouds, and fometimes projecting fo far over the road, as feeming to impede our farther progrefs : the wide expanfe of the ocean, in front, with the arm of the fea running up the country in the centre of the valley; in fine, the *tout enfemble* claimed our higheft admiration.

Barmouth, though confidered as a bathing-place, is very inferior to Tenby, yet its fituation for grandeur of rocks, has been frequently compared, by many Tourifts, to Gibraltar ; and by others, efteemed not unlike St. Kitts, in the Weft Indies. The vaft fand banks, formed by the tides immediately in front of the town, are the only barriers which protect it from the inundations of the fea. The fhore is extremely level, and affords, for many miles, excellent riding. In refpect to the bathing, little can be faid to recommend it ; the machines are not drawn into the water, and by this palpable inconvenience, you are under the difagreeable

agreeable neceffity of walking a confiderable way in, before the water is fufficiently deep for " plunging " headlong in the briny flood." During our ftay here, two gentlemen perceiving that the water was very much alloyed by a frefh water ftream difembogaing itfelf into the fea, at Barmouth, perfuaded Mrs. Lewis, the obliging landlady of the Cors-y-gedol Arms, to remove the machines farther from the town; and from them we were informed, that though the falt water was purer, yet they found it impoffible to draw them fufficiently deep for good bathing : the machines being ftationary on the fands, the ladies likewife find it remarkably inconvenient, being equally compelled to walk in. The folly of this method feems to be more ftriking, as the objection might be fo eafily obviated. The lower clafs here, as in many other parts of Wales, indifcriminately drefs and undrefs on the fands, and pay very little diftinction to their fex.

The board and lodging is regulated on the fame excellent plan here as at Tenby, with very little difference in refpect to the expence. The town itfelf is very dirty, and fo irregularly built, on the declivity of a rock, that the windows of one houfe not uncommonly look down on the neighbouring chimney. We could not avoid obferving the number of pigs, which are efteemed in this part of the country far fuperior to

G 4　　　　　　any

any in England, lying in every corner of the ſtreet; and theſe pigs, I rather imagine, conſider themſelves, during the night, inmates of the peaſant's cottage: yet theſe hardſhips, if they may be diſtinguiſhed by that name, the inhabitants of the hovel ſuffer without complaint, and deem themſelves perfectly happy as long as they poſſeſs a pile of turf to keep off the inclemency of the winter's blaſt, a ſmall ſtrip of ground, well ſtocked with potatoes, ſome poultry, and a fat pig; though one hovel protects them all.   Though to appearance, their ſituation is moſt miſerable, yet it has no effect on their tempers and diſpoſitions; their hoſpitality, and indeed kindneſs, towards ſtrangers in diſtreſs, is an intereſting trait in their character: to inſtance this, I am induced to mention an anecdote, which took place at Hubberſtone, not long ago.   A lady anxiouſly waiting the arrival of her huſband, from Ireland, at the miſerable village of Hubberſtone, ſoon intereſted even the meaner inhabitants of the place in her behalf; who willing to render her ſituation as comfortable as poſſible, ſeemed to vie with each other in producing the moſt delicious fruits, and the choiceſt garlands of flowers, to preſent them to the unhappy conſort; and not content alone with this, ſhe was generally greeted in the ſtreets, with the phraſe, "There goes poor "Mrs. L——." The lady, at laſt, impatient for the arrival of her huſband, determined to ſail for Ireland.

The

The faithfulnefs of the little group that accompanied her to the fhore, can better be imagined than defcribed; the laft farewell, with tears of artlefs innocence, and the befeeching that Providence " who governs the " waves, and ftills the raging of the fea," to grant her a profperous voyage; all this feemed to come fo thoroughly from the bottom of their hearts, that we cannot avoid feeling ourfelves interefted in their behalf.

The road from hence to

HARLECH,

is ftony and uninterefting; to the left an unbounded view of the wide ocean, and in front, the fteep mountains of North Wales rofe in endlefs perfpective. About four miles from Barmouth, we paffed the two lodges at Tal-y-bont, leading to Cors-y-gedol, the feat of Sir Thomas Moftyn. It is practicable to go by the fands, but we were given to underftand, by Mrs. Lewis, that the turnpike was, if any thing, fhorter, the fcenery more pleafing, and the guides neceffary for croffing thofe dangerous fands, in general, moft complete villains.

Harlech, though formed by Edward I. into a borough, can now be efteemed little more than a dirty
village:

village : the prefent caftle, one of the moft entire in
Wales, is founded on a very high rock, projecting in
the Irifh Sea, and defended by a deep fofs on the eaft
fide ; below it is a marfh of confiderable extent, occafionally overflowed by the fea ; from the top of the
walls to this marfh the height is very confiderable, and
from thence the Bay of Cardigan is feen to great advantage ; in addition to this, the fhagged fummits
of Cader Buchan and Snowdon, in Caernarvonfhire,
being inveloped in clouds, appear fcarcely vifible.

At the public-houfe, we accidentally met with a
well-informed man, who minutely delineated every
part of the caftle ; beginning with the founder, in the
true characteriftic ftyle of a Welchman, run through
his pedigree feveral generations : this, however, did
not intereft us, curfory pedeftrians ; and with little
perfuafion we foon induced him to write down, in as
concife a manner as poffible, any information he was
acquainted with refpecting the caftle : " The founder
" of Harlech Caftle, A. D. 552, was Maclegwynn ;
" Gwynead made Caer Dugoll (Shrewfbury ;) Caer
" Gyffin (Aber Conway ;) Caer Gollwyn (Harleck)
" fuppofed to be buried in Cirefter, and reigned thirty-
" four years." Whether this information is correct, I
will not take upon me to affert ; but meeting with a
Welchman, in this part of the country, capable of
writing,

writing, rather furprifed us, and induced me to tranfcribe this fhort paragraph.

The double gate-way, with four ftrong towers, is
ftill very perfect; and the whole in fufficient repair, to
form a conjecture of its ancient extent and grandeur.
It was originally fuppofed to have been a Roman town,
a conjecture founded on the great number of coins, and
other pieces of antiquity, which have been found here,
and in the neighbourhood.

In 1408 it was taken by the Earl of Pembroke; and
afforded likewife fhelter to Margaret of Anjour, after
the battle of Northampton, 1460, and was the laft in
North-Wales, which held out for the King, being fur-
rendered to General Mytton, 1647.

In a garden near this caftle was dug up, in the year
1692, an antient golden torques, of a round form, an
inch in circumference, and weighing eight ounces.
This curious relick of Britifh antiquity, exhibited in
a drawing by Mr. Pennant, ftill continues in the
poffeffion of the Moftyn family. As we had not an
opportunity of examining the original, this account
can only be gathered from the information of former
authors, who reprefent it, as " a wreathed bar, or ra-
" ther three or four rods twifted together, about four
" feet

" feet long, flexible, but bending naturally only one
" way, in form of a hat-band : it originally had holes
" at each end, not twisted or sharp, but plain, and cut
" even."

In 1694, the prodigious phenomenon of fire, or
kindled exhalation, which disturbed the inhabitants of
this neighbourhood, is both singular and extraordinary; sixteen ricks of hay, and two barns, were burnt by
a kindled exhalation, or blue weak flame, proceeding
from the sea: this lasted about a fortnight or three
weeks, poisoning the grass, and firing it for the space of
a mile.   It is extraordinary, that it had no effect on
the men, who interposed their endeavours to save the
ricks from destruction, even by running into it.   For
a more accurate account of this singular phenomenon,
I refer my readers to the *Philosophical Transactions*,
No. 208, and likewise to the Addenda, in Cambden :
suffice it to say, that the air and grass was so infected,
that it occasioned a great mortality of cattle, horses,
sheep, and goats.   The various conjectures that have
been formed, to account for this kindled exhalation,
seem to be very unsatisfactory ; something similar to
this, both in the appearance and in the effect, happened
in France in the year 1734.

As, from the unfavourableness of the weather, we
had

had not contemplated the rich fcenery between Barmouth and Dolgelly, with that nice inveftigation which it deferved, we determined, by again returning to our obliging landlady at the Cors-y-gedol Arms, to feize the opportunity of again admiring its beauties; and, by taking a more circuitous route to the Vale of Feftiniog, pay that attention to the Falls of Doll-y-mullin, Moddach, and Caen, which they fo defervedly require.

This fecond faunter we found by no means tedious: the fcene feemed perpetually changing at every unexpected curvature of the road; and the rude features of the mountains appeared to affume new forms, as the winding prefented them to the eye in different attitudes, whilft the fhifting vapours, which partially concealed their minuter grandeur, affifted the illufions of the fight. Amidft new woods, rifing in the majefty of foliage, the fcattered cottage, with its bluifh fmoke curling high in the air, was frequently rendered interefting by its neat fimplicity: and ferved to conftitute the romantic beauties of this picturefque faunter.

This pleafing fcenery varied little till we arrived within two miles of Dolgelly, when feveral gentlemens' feats burft upon our fight; and leaving that enchanting fpot to the left, at the Laneltyd turnpike, a different object pre-

presented itself to our view. For four miles we walked
by the side of a hill, the most translucent stream attending us the whole way; for though the road was situated
so much above it, yet the sandy bottom, with the
finny tribe, in considerable numbers, sporting in this
transparent element, were easily descried. On each
side, the mountains rose to a considerable height,
with the craggy summit of Cader Idris claiming the
pre-eminence. We soon arrived at the small ale-house
(Traveller's Rest) where we met the labourer of Mr.
Madox, whom we were recommended to enquire for,
as a proper ciceroni to the water-falls in his vicinity.
Having finished our scanty but wholesome repast, we
repaired with an old woman, the labourer being confined to the house by indisposition, to the fall of Doll-
y-mullin. There appeared to be something singular in
the appearance of this " mountain elf;" destitute of
shoes and stockings, in the true Cambrian stile, she
trip'd it, occasionally singing, and sometimes discon-
tented with the world, herself, and every thing, utter-
ing a most dismal groan. This excited our curiosity;
but to learn much of her situation we soon found im-
practicable; her knowledge of the English language
was very trivial; and as she seemed not much inclined
to give us any information respecting the adjacent
country, we found it useless to make enquiries concerning her condition in life.

Our

Our furly conductrefs firſt led us through Mr. Madox's grounds; to the left of the Tan-y-bwlch road, by
a moſt delightful walk cut through the wood, we now
foon reached the falls of Doll-y-mullin, the roaring of
which had a long time announced its vicinity. This
cataract, though confidered only as a prelude to the
grand falls of the Cayne and Moddach, is ſtill worthy
the attention of the paſſing traveller; for though the
river precipitates itſelf not more than fifty feet, yet the
projection and fituation of the rocks, and the thick oak,
carelefsly throwing its broad brown arms acrofs the
troubled waters, is fingularly pleafing. We had hitherto
only contemplated this ſcene from the foot of the fall;
but how noble the effect, when we began to wind up
the ſteep afcent, and paufed at every bafon, which the
water had formed in the excavated rock.

By a retrograde faunter we foon gained the Tan-y-
bwlch road, and paſſing over the romantic bridge of
Pont ar Garfa, beautifully entwined with the rich drapery of ivy, we afcended a ſteep path over the flaty
mountain of Tylyn Gwladys, two miles in extent.—
Sublimity, indeed, gave place to elegance; behind us,
the huge ſteeps of Cader Idris, lifting high above the
rolling clouds its fhaggy head, of which at intervals,
we caught a glance through the thick miſt which enveloped it; in front Snowdon, confcious of pre-eminence,
                                                        rofe

rose in the diftant perfpective; thefe were the boundaries of our view. On the oppofite fide a barren mountain, dignified by the name of Prince of Wales, appeared fcarcely acceffible, but to the fteps of the enthufiaft; this formerly afforded a vaft quantity of ore, but it has lately fo much failed, as not to produce even a fufficiency to remunerate the miners. While traverfing thefe barren mountains, it is not lefs fingular than in-terefting, occafionally to meet the moft delicious vallies, watered by fome foaming river; thefe literally fur-charged

"With weighted rains, and melted Alpine fnows."

Such is the true characteriftic of the Welch fcenery: the fineft verdure, and the moft enchanting vallies are difcovered in the bofom of fterility, where natural caf-cades, precipitating themfelves from their rude pinna-cles, alone difturb the filence which reigns in that afylum, only to render it more enchanting to the inqui-fitive pedeftrians, for thefe landfcapes are only acceffible to their fteps: the diftant fwell of the cataract had now long proclaimed our proximity to the object in purfuit. The falls of the Cayne and the Moddach are at no great diftance from one another, being only feparated by a thick wood. Croffing a fmall bridge, above fifty feet from the water, formed only by the trunk of an oak, which has accidentally fallen acrofs the rapid torrent;

. our

our conductrefs very judicioufly felected the latter as the firft object for our admiration. The computed meafurement of this fall is eftimated between feventy and eighty feet, dividing itfelf into three diftinct parts, each finely broken by the projected rocks : the quantity of water is very inconfiderable; but the whole is admirably prefented to the eye in one view. The firft fall, about twenty feet, precipitates itfelf into a deep pool, thirty feet diameter ; from thence over a fecond ledge, thirty feet high ; and, laftly, it difcharges itfelf into a pool of confiderable dimenfions. The declivities of the rocks are luxuriantly clothed with wood ; the oak more particularly fpreading its gigantic arms acrofs the foaming torrent : a variety of trees, indeed, profufely embellifh the whole of this glen, which are finely contrafted with the dark brown rocks; conftituting fo finifhed a picture, and reprefenting fuch a variety of colours, that their beauties the imagination can better conceive, than the pen defcribe.

We now returned to the fall of the Cayne, infinitely fuperior to any in Wales, being two hundred feet perpendicular, uninterrupted by rocks, and not intercepted by the thick wood which encircles it. For a confiderable time we both of us gazed with that wrapt admiration, which loathes to be difturbed by the mutual exchange of our ideas; and ftunned with the continual

H   uproar,

uproar, and never-ceasing tumultous motion of the sparkling foam, we silently admired the grandeur of the landscape. On each side the horrific crags seemed to bid defiance to the goat's activity. The Cayne, after this stunning cataract, throws its troubled waters over a rocky bed, till it unites itself with the Moddach below.

With reluctance we left this romantic situation; and, according to the directions of our conductress, soon found ourselves in the turnpike road to Tan-y-bwlch, understanding that Mr. Warner's route to Pen-street afforded indifferent walking. Stupendous mountains attended us some way; and, to borrow a description from a celebrated author, they " looked like the rude mate- " rials of creation, forming the barrier of unwrought " space." The sun was now making a " golden " set;" the mountains were thrown together in noble masses, appearing to scale the heavens, to intercept its rays, and emulous to receive the parting tinge of lingering day. We were watching with admiration the mild splendor of its light, fading from the distant landscape, when we perceived the rich vale of Festiniog suddenly open itself to our view : we observed the busy group of haymakers, who had compleated their day's labour, returning to their homes :

" While

" While heard from dale to dale,
" Waking the breeze, refounds the blended voice
" Of happy labour, love and focial glee."

Pleafed with this ruftic fcene, we caught the cheerful
fong, which was wafted on the gentle breeze. With
pleafure we anticipated a faunter through this vale,
early the enfuing morning; for one tint of fober gray
had now covered its various coloured features, and the
fun had now gleamed its laft light upon the rivulet
which winds through the bottom.

TAN-Y-BWLCH.

The " rich-hair'd youth of morn" had not long left
its faffron bed, and the very air was balmy as it frefh-
ened into morn, when we hurried from our Inn to
enjoy the luxuries of the Vale of Feftiniog, fo well
celebrated by the pen of Lord Littleton. " With the
" woman one loves, with the friend of one's heart,
" (fays his Lordfhip) and a good ftudy of books, one
" may pafs an age there, and think it a day. If one
" has a mind to live long, and renew his youth, let
" him come and fettle at Feftiniog." Thefe are the
fentiments of Lord Littleton, in which feemed to be
verified the fituation of Mr. Oakley, who has felected
this fpot for his refidence. Tan-y-bwlch Hall, (for

H 2   by

by that name is Mr. Oakley's Seat dignified) is environed by a thick wood, which climbs the steep
mountains behind his mansion. We followed the
meandering and tranflucent waters of the river Dryryd,
till we arrived at the Village of Maentwrog, fituated
about the middle of this Paradife. Paffing through the
village, we obferved a fmall but neat cottage, which
was rendered interefting to the way-farer by its neat
fimplicity. Perceiving a ftand of fruit at the door,
we were enticed to enter the cottage, where we found
the interior of the houfe as comfortable, as the fituation was interefting. A large old-fafhioned chimney corner, with benches to receive a focial party,
formed a moft enviable retreat from the rude ftorms of
winter, and defied alike the weather and the world :—
with what pleafure did I picture,

     " A fmiling circle, emulous to pleafe,"

gathering round a blazing pile of wood on the hearth,
free from all the viciffitudes and cares of the world,
happy in their own home, bleffed in the fweet affec-
tions of kindred amity, regardlefs of the winter blaft
that ftruggled againft the window, and the fnow that
pelted againft the roof. On our entering, the wife
who poffeffed " the home of happinefs, an honeft
" breaft," invited us " to take a feat" under the window, which overlooking the village, and the dark
                          tower

tower of the church, offered the delights of other fea-
fons. The fweets of a little garden, joined its fragrance to the honeyfuckle, which enwreathed with rich
drapery the windows; and here too lay the old family
Bible, which had been put afide on our firft entrance:
we regretted, not having an opportunity of feeing the
hufband, whom, I make no doubt

   " Envied not, and never thought of kings,
   " Nor from thofe appetites fuftain'd annoy,
   " That chance may fruftrate, or indulgence cloy;
   " Each feafon look'd delightful as it paft,
   " To the fond hufband, and the faithful wife."

Our intended route for this day being very fhort, we
did not leave Tan-y-bwlch till after breakfaft, and even
then lingered through the valley, to take one laft adieu of
this paradifiacal fpot; the Dryryd ferpentizing through
the meadows, and the lively green of the fwelling declivities on each fide, beautifully contrafted with the
ripening corn. From the vaft quantity of ore we difcovered, I am inclined to believe, that any fpirited fpe-
culator would find it amply repay him for the expences
and labour attending his fpeculations. The vale of
Feftiniog, not exceeding three miles long, and one in
breadth, is a very rich tract of land.

An extremely rough, rocky, and unpleafant road,
H 3   with

with nothing to engage our attention; and the country uncultivated, and divefted of every thing that gives, even the fhadow of civilization, brought us to the far-famed Pont Aber-glaflyn, or, *The Bridge of the Harbour of the Blue Lake*; and not uncommonly ftiled, the *Devil's Bridge*. This laft appellation has very frequently mifled ftrangers, who, confounding it with the well-known bridge at Havod, have been much difappointed, their expectations being raifed very high, from the general defcriptions of that place. Of this, indeed, we found an inftance on the very fpot. This bridge connects the two counties of Merionethfhire and Caernarvonfhire; being, from the parapet to the water, forty feet. From the defcription of former tourifts, it did not anfwer our expectations; but the falmon-leap is an interefting object from the bridge : the height is about fifteen feet; and though we obferved very many attempt this furprifing feat of agility, not one fucceeded. Some fifhermen below foon excited our curiofity, and falmon was here offered for fale at three-pence per pound.

An intelligent man here offered himfelf as our guide to the rich Copper-mines, in the vicinity of Pont Aber-Glaflyn. This miner, having worked both here and at the Paris mountain, confidently afferted, that one pound of this ore was now efteemed equivalent to twice the quantity, produced in Anglefea. Stupendous cliffs,

cliffs, by the road fide, literally rife eight hundred and fixty feet perpendicularly, and hang in the moft capricious forms over the torrent, which, ftraggling amongft the receffes of ftone, is haftening forward to difembogue itfelf into the eftuary of Traeth Mawr. The pafs is not more than feventy feet; after much rain it is entirely inundated by the overflowings of the Glaflyn, which reflected, as in a mirror, the blacknefs of the impending cliffs. On the Caernarvonfhire fide are feveral lead mines; but they have not proved fufficiently rich, to reward the labour of working.

The fituation of our Inn at

BEDDGELERT,

is very romantic, and would form an interefting drawing, by taking in a fmall bridge of two arches below the houfe. It is completely encircled by lofty mountains, which may be confidered as fubject to the " cloud- " capt Snowdon."

How often has the idea of this ftupendous mountain filled my heart with enthufiaftic rapture! Every time I caft my eyes on that folemn, that majeftic vifion, it is not without the moft powerful emotion; it excites that

H 4

tender

tender melancholy, which exalts, rather than depreffes the mind ! How delightful, to bid adieu to all the cares and occupations of the world, for the reflection of thofe fcenes of fublimity and grandeur, which forms fuch contraft to the tranfientnefs of fublunary greatnefs ! With what anxiety have we watched the fetting fun, loitering juft below the horizon, and illuminating the higheft fummit of Snowdon with a golden tinge, and we ftill watch the paffing clouds of night, fearing left the morning fhould prove unfavourable for our Alpine excurfion.

SNOWDON.

We engaged the Miner, as our Conductor over the mountain, who entertained us much with difplaying, in ftrong colours, the tricks and impofitions of his bro- ther guides, and more particularly of the methodiftical Landlord of our Inn, who is generally employed on thefe occafions. His pride too is not a little elevated, by having conducted *The Great Doctor* to its higheft fum- mit ; this feemingly ridiculous phrafe for fome time puzzled us; but we have fince found out, that our guide was talking of no lefs a man, than the prefent refpectable and learned Dean of Chriftchurch, who
afcended

afcended this mountain laft year. Though our guide*
was pompous, and rather too partial to the marvellous,
yet I ftrenuoufly recommend him to all tourifts.

At half paft twelve, we ftarted from our Inn, determined to fee the fun rife from its higheft fummit. The
night was now very dark, and we could juft difcover,
that the top of Snowdon was entirely enveloped in a
thick, impenetrable mift: this unpropitious omen ftag-
gered our refolutions; and we for fome time hefitated refpecting our farther progrefs; but our guide affuring us,
that his *comfortable* cottage was not far diftant, we again
plucked up refolution; and quitting the highway about
two miles on the Caernarvon road, we turned to the
right, through a boggy unpleafant land, and in danger
of lofing our fhoes every ftep we took. This foon
brought us to the *comfortable cot*, the filth and dirtinefs
of which can better be imagined than defcribed; a
worm-eaten bed, two fmall ftools, and a table fixed to
the wall, compofed the whole of his furniture,—two
fighting cocks were perched on a beam, which Thomas
feemed to pride himfelf in the poffeffion of; the fmoke
of the fire afcended through a fmall hole in the roof of
this *comfortable manfion*, the door of which did not ap-

* Evan Thomas, works in the copper-works at Aber-Glaflyn, and lives
at a place called Dous Coreb, about a mile and an half beyond Beddgelert.

pear

pear proof againſt the "churliſh chiding of the winter "blaſt."

Such, indeed, was the ſituation of this Cambrian mountaineer; and though, in our own opinion, miſery, poverty, and dirt perſonified, ſeemed to be the real inhabitants of this cottage, yet there was ſomething prepoſſeſſing in his character; for frequently, with the greateſt vehemence imaginable, and in the true ſtile of an anchorite, he declared, that "though he boaſted "not riches, yet he boaſted of independence; and "though he poſſeſſed not wealth, yet he poſſeſſed the "home of happineſs, an honeſt breaſt."

The morning appearing to wear a more favourable aſpect, we again ſallied forth; the bogs, however, ſtill rendered it extremely unpleaſant. But this inconvenience was only temporary : we ſoon came to a part of the mountain, entirely compoſed of looſe ſtones, and fragments of rock, which, by affording a very treacherous footing, you are liable to perpetual falls. The mountain now became much ſteeper, the path leſs rocky, and our mountaineer, the higher we proceeded, more induced to exhibit feats of his agility, by occaſionally running down a ſhort precipice, and then, by a loud ſhout or vociferation, ſhewing us the obedience of the ſheep, who inſtantaneouſly flocked round him, at the

found

found of his voice : it is fingular, the caution implanted in this animal, by inftinct, for the mutual protection of each other; from the liberty they enjoy, they feldom congregate in one flock, but are generally difcovered grazing in parties from fix to a dozen, one of which is regularly appointed centinel, to watch the motions of their inveterate enemies (foxes and birds of prey), which infeft this mountain. A wider expanfe of the hemifphere difclofed itfelf, and every object below us gradually diminifhed, as we afcended. The frefhnefs of the mountain *whetted* our appetites ; and our conductor, with very little perfuafion, foon influenced us to open our little bafket of provifions. The fun, the " rich-hair'd youth of morn," was juft peeping from its bed ; and having refrefhed ourfelves, with eager impatience we again climbed the rugged precipice, for we had ftill a confiderable height to afcend. We now defcended feveral fteep declivities, by a narrow path, not more than three yards wide, with a dreadful perpendicular on each fide, the fight of which almoft turned us giddy. As we were paffing this hazardous path, a thick mift enveloped us, and an impenetrable abyfs appeared on both fides ; the effect, indeed, can fcarcely be conceived ; our footing to us, puifne mountaineers, feemed very infecure ; and a total deftruction would have been the confequence of one falfe ftep. The air grew intenfely cold, and by our guide's recommendation,

tion, we a second time produced our piftol of rum, diluted with milk; but this cordial muft be ufed with caution, as a very fmall quantity of ftrong liquor affects the head, owing to the rarification of the air. On our reaching the fummit, all our difficulties were forgotten, and our imaginary complaints overborne with exclamations of wonder, furprife, and admiration. The light thin mifty cloud, which had for fome time enveloped us, as if by enchantment, fuddenly difperfed; the whole ocean appeared illuminated by a fiery fubftance, and all the fubject hills below us, for they refembled *mole-hills*, were gradually tinged by the rich glow of the fun; whofe orb, becoming at length diftinctly vifible, difplayed the whole ifland of Anglefea fo diftinctly, that we defcried, as in map, its flat and uncultivated plains, bounded by the rich and inexhauftible Paris Mountains, in the vicinity of Holyhead. The point on which we were ftanding, did not exceed a fquare of five yards, and we fickened almoft at the fight of the fteep precipices which environed us; round it is a fmall parapet, formed by the cuftomary tribute of all ftrangers, who vifit this fummit, and to which we likewife contributed, by placing a large ftone on its top: this parapet, indeed, fheltered us from the chilly cold, and protected us from the piercing wind, which this height muft naturally be expofed to.

We

We remained in this situation for a considerable time, and endeavoured, without success, to enumerate the several lakes, forest, woods, and counties, which were exposed to us in one view; but, lost and confounded with the innumerable objects worthy of admiration, and regardless of the chilling cold, we took a distinct survey of the Isle of Man, together with a faint prospect of the highlands in Ireland, which appeared just visibly skirting the distant horizon; but another object soon engrossed all our attention;

"" The wide, the unbounded prospects lay before us;
"" But shadows, clouds, and darkness rest upon it :"

For we unexpectedly observed long billows of vapour tossing about, half way down the mountain, totally excluding the country below, and occasionally dispersing, and partially revealing, its features, while above, the azure expanse of the heavens remained unobscured by the thinnest mist. This, however, was of no long continuance : a thick cloud presently wet us through ; and the point on which we were standing could alone be distinguished. As there appeared little or no chance of the clouds dispersing, we soon commenced our descent.—Respecting this Alpine excursion, suffice it to say, that though our expectations were raised exceedingly high, it infinitely surpassed all conception, and baffled all description ; for no colour of
lan-

language can paint the grandeur of the rifing fun, obferved from this eminence, or defcribe the lakes, woods, and forefts, which are extended before you; for defcription, though it enumerates their names, yet it cannot draw the elegance of outline, cannot give the effect of precipices, or delineate the minute features, which reward the actual obferver, at every new choice of his pofition, and by changing their colour and form in his gradual afcent, till at laft every object dwindles into atoms : in fhort, this interefting excurfion, which comprehends every thing that is awful, grand, and fublime, producing the moft pleafing fenfations, has left traces in the memory, which the imagination will ever hold dear.

Various have been the conjectures on the definition of this mountain ; fome authors affirm, that the Welch name of Snowdon fignifies the *Eagle's Rocks*, deducing it from the number of thofe birds that formerly haunted thefe rocks ; but the moft fimple conjecture feems to be, that this name alludes to the frequency of the fnow on the higheft peaks. This monntainous tract was formerly celebrated for its fertility and woods ; and Leland affirms, that all Crigereri was foreft. It now yields no corn; and its produce confifts in cattle and black fheep, with large flocks of goats. " Its height " (fays Pennant) has been varioufly reported. Mr. Caf-

well,

" well, who was employed by Mr. Adams, in a furvey
" of Wales, 1682, meafured it by inftruments, made
" by the direction of Mr. Flamftead, and afferts it to
" have been one thoufand two hundred and forty. Mr.
Lluyd fays, its perpendicular height is about one thou-
" fand three hundred yards above the fea level; but
" later experiments have afcertained it at one thoufand
" one hundred and eighty-nine yards, reckoning from
" the quay at Caernarvon, to the higheft peak." The
afcent is computed three miles; the extremity, or fummit, three quarters of a mile perpendicular. By the inhabitants of the country it is called Moel-y-Wydva, *i. e.*
The Confpicuous Hill; and fometimes Krag Ey reri; and
in the old Englifh maps it is always fpelt *Snawdon.*
The lakes in this tract amount to a confiderable number, and abound with trout, eels, gwyniadd, and fome
of them well-ftored with char. The moft noted peaks
of this mountain are diftinguifhed by the names Moel-
y-Wydva, y-Glyder, Karmedh Dhavidh, and Karmedh Llewelyn.——Thefe hills are, in a manner, heaped
on one another, near the fummit; and we only climbed
one rock, to fee three or four more; between each is a
cwm, or valley, generally with a lake. We made particular enquiries concerning y-Glyder-Bach, and found
that the defcription of it is by no means exaggerated.
Several columnar ftones, of enormous fize, formed into
the moft fantaftical fhapes, and lying in feveral directions,

tions, with many of their tops crowned with ſtonss, placed horizontally on them. One we obſerved rocked with the ſlighteſt touch. In the fiſſures of the rock, *cubic pyritæ*, are not uncommonly found; the *ſaxifraga nivalis*, and the ſpecies called by Linnæus *æthereal*, in great abundance.

The firſt two miles of our deſcent, we by no means found difficult, but wiſhing to take a minute ſurvey of the picturefque paſs of Llanberris, we changed the route generally preſcribed to ſtrangers, and deſcended a rugged and almoſt perpendicular path, in oppoſition to the propoſals of our guide, who ſtrenuouſly endeavoured to diſſuade us from the attempt, alleging the difficulty of the ſteep, and relating a melancholy ſtory of a gentleman, who many years back had broken his leg. This had no effect. We determined to proceed; and the vale of Llanberris amply rewarded us for the trouble. It is bounded by the ſteep precipices of Snowdon, and two large lakes, communicating by a river. It was formerly a large foreſt, but the woods are now entirely cut down. We here diſmiſſed our Cambrian mountaineer, and eaſily found our way to Dolbadern (pronounced *Dolbathern*) Caſtle, ſituated between the two lakes, and now reduced to one circular tower, thirty feet in diameter, with the foundations of the exterior buildings completely in ruins; in this, Owen Gough,

brother

brother to Llewellin, laft prince, was confined in prifon. From hence a rugged horfe-path brought us to
the Caernarvon turnpike-road, about fix miles diftant ;
the high towers of the caftle, the very crown and paragon
of the landfcape, at laft pointed out the fituation of

CAERNARVON ;

and having croffed a handfome modern ftone-bridge,
thrown over the river Rhydol, and built by " Harry
" Parry, the modern Inigo, *Anno Domini* 1791," we
foon entered this antient town, very much fatigued with
our long excurfion. The Hotel, newly built by Lord
Uxbridge, for the convenience of ftrangers, at the end
of the town, commands a fine profpect of the Strait
of Menai. The view was bounded by the flat Ifle of
Anglefea ; while the light veffels, fkimming before the
wind, gave the whole a lively and pleafing variety.

The city of Caernavon, beautifully fituated, and regularly built, is in the form of a fquare, enclofed on
three fides, with thick ftone walls ; and on the fouth
fide, defended by the caftle ;—the old town-hall is now
falling to ruin.

With refpect to the caftle, we by no means agree
with Mr. Warner, that " its high antiquity and an-

I   " tient

" tient fplendor is interrupted and deftroyed by the
" patch-work of modern feparation, and the littlenefs
" of a cottager's domeftic œconomy feen within its
" walls;" as it is only repaired, where neceffity re-
quired it, to prop up its crumbling ruins; neither
could we difcover any cottage within its walls. The
towers are extremely elegant; but not being entwined
with ivy, do not wear that picturefque appearance,
which caftles generally poffefs. Over the principal
entrance, which leads into an oblong court, is feated,
beneath a great tower, the ftatue of the founder, holding in his left hand a dagger: this gate-way was originally fortified with four portcullifes. At the weft end,
the eagle tower, remarkably light and beautiful, in
a polygon form; three fmall hexagon turrets rifing
from the middle, with eagles placed on their battlements; from thence it derives its name. In a little
dark room* in this tower, meafuring eleven feet by feven, was born Edward the Second, April 25, 1204.
The thicknefs of the wall is about ten feet.. To the
top of the tower we reckoned one hundred and fifty-
eight fteps, from whence an extenfive view of the adjacent country is feen to great advantage. On the fouth
are three octagonal towers with fmall turrets, with

---

* Such is the received opinion; but the place noted for this event, is
only a thoroughfare to the grand apartments of the tower, the middle one
of which appears more probably to have been the room.

fimilar

fimilar ones on the north. All thefe towers communicate with each other by a gallery, both on the ground, middle, and upper floor, formed within the immenfe thicknefs of the walls, in which are cut narrow flips, at convenient diftances, for the difcharge of arrows.

This building founded on a rock, is the work of Edward I. the conqueror of the principality ; the form of it is a long irregular fquare, enclofing an area of about two acres and a half. From the information of the Sebright manufcript, Mr. Pennant fays, that by the united efforts of the peafants, it was erected within the fpace of one year.

Having fpent near three hours furveying one of the nobleft caftles in Wales, we walked round the environs of the town : the terrace round the caftle walls is exceedingly pleafing, being in front of the Menai, which is here upwards of a mile in breadth, forming a fafe harbour for craft of five or fix tons, and generally crowded with veffels, exhibiting a picture of national induftry; whilft near it a commodious quay prefents an ever-buftling fcene, from whence a confiderable quantity of flate, and likewife copper from the Llanberris mine, is fhipped for different parts of the kingdom.

Caer-

Caernarvon may certainly be confidered as one of the handfomeft and largeft towns in North-Wales; and under the patronage of Lord Uxbridge promifes to become ftill more populous and extenfive: his Lordfhip, we were given to underftand by our landlord, intends to erect fea-baths; and by this well-planned improvement, induce company to refort here during the fummer months.

Several excurfions may be made from Caernarvon with great fatisfaction to the Tourift; the principal of which is a vifit to

PLAS-NEWYDD,

the elegant feat of Lord Uxbridge, fituated in the Ifle of Anglefey, and diftant about fix miles from Caernarvon: if the wind and tide prove favorable, the picturefque fcenery of the Menai, will be viewed to great advantage, by hiring a boat at the quay.* But if this moft advifeable plan fhould not be approved of, the walk to the Mol-y-don Ferry, about five miles on the Bangor road, will prove highly gratifying: the Menai, whofe banks are ftudded with gentlemens' feats, appearing fcarcely vifible between the rich foliage of the oak, which luxu-

* The hire of a boat from feven fhillings and fix-pence to half-a-guinea.

riates

riates to the water's brink, is filled with veſſels, whoſe
gay ſtreamers, glittering to the ſun-beam, preſent to
the eye a conſtant, moving object ; whilſt the voice of
the ſailors, exchanging ſome ſalute with the paſſing
veſſel, is gently wafted on the breeze.

Croſſing the ferry, we ſoon reached the antient reſidence of the Arch-Druid of Britain, and where was
formerly ſtationed the moſt celebrated of the antient Bri-
tiſh Academies ; from this circumſtance, many places in
this iſland ſtill retain their original appellation, as *Myſy-
rim*, the Place of Studies ; *Caer Edris*, the City of
Aſtronomy; *Cerrig Boudyn*, the Aſtronomer's Circle.
The ſhore to the right ſoon brought us to the Plantations of Plâs-Newydd, conſiſting chiefly of the moſt venerable oaks, and nobleſt aſh in this part of the country.

  ———." Superior to the pow'r
 " Of all the warring winds of heaven they riſe ;
 " And from the ſtormy promontory tower,
 " And toſs their giant arms amid the ſkies ;
 " While each aſſailing blaſt increaſing ſtrength ſupplies."
       BEATTIE's *Minſtrel.*

Beneath their " broad brown" branches, we diſcovered ſeveral *cromlechs*, the monuments of Druidical
ſuperſtition ; ſeveral ſtones of enormous ſize ſupport

    I 3   two

two others placed horizontally over them.*   For what purpofe thefe antient relicks were originally erected, it was not for us puifne antiquarians to difcufs, and with eager impatience we hurried to vifit the noble manfion, which has not yet received the finifhing ftroke of the architect; fufficient however is accomplifhed to form a conjecture of its intended fplendor and magnificence. The whole is built, ftables included, in a Gothic caftellated form, of a dark flate-coloured ftone ; on entering the veftibule, we, for a fhort time, imagined our-felves in the chapel, a miftake, though foon difcovered, yet liable to happen to any vifitor; the ceiling having Gothic arches, with a gallery fuitable to it, and feveral niches cut in the fide walls : we were next conducted through a long fuite of apartments, the defign of them all equally convenient and elegant. The landfcape from the Gothic windows is both beautiful and fublime; a noble plantation of trees, the growth of ages——the winding ftrait of the Menai, gay with veffels paffing and repaffing; and beyond this tranquil fcene, the long range of the Snowdon mountains fhooting into the clouds, the various hues of whofe features appear as beautiful, as their magnitude is fublime.   The houfe is protected

---

* " The eaftern feems originally to have confifted of feven ftones, fix " uprights fupporting an immenfe fuperincumbent one, (with its flat " face lying upon them) thirteen feet long, nearly as much broad, and " four feet thick."——WARNER's *Second Walk.*

from

from the encroachment of the fea, by a ftrong parapet embattled wall; in fine, this magnificent feat of Lord Uxbridge, feems to poffefs many conveniencies peculiar to its fituation: the warm and cold baths, conftantly filled by the Menai, are fequeftered and commodious, and every apartment of the houfe is abundantly fupplied with water.*

Being unavoidably prevented vifiting the celebrated Paris mountain, the property of Lord Uxbridge and the Rev. Mr. Hughes, we again returned to the Hotel, at Caernarvon, purporting to ftay the following day, (Sunday) for the purpofe of making a ftrict enquiry into the religious fect, fettled here, and in many parts of Wales, called *Jumpers.*† The account we had received from our landlord, we imagined was

---

* In the time of the Romans, this ifland was called, by the Britons, *Mona*; but becoming fubject to the Englifh, in the time of Egbert, it was afterwards termed *Anglefea*, or the Englifhman's Ifland. See ROWLAND's *Mon. Ant.* p. 172, 173.

† Before the Author of this Itinerary propofed publifhing this Tour through the Cambrian territories, he was induced to fend an account of this extraordinary fect to the Gentleman's Magazine, (July, 1799, p. 579.) This is, therefore, only to be confidered as a repetition; with the addition of a brief extract from the two fubfequent letters, (September, 1799, p. 741, and November, p. 938,) given to the public by different hands, through the medium of the Gentleman's Magazine.

I 4

exag-

exaggerated, and this more ſtrongly induced us to viſit the chapel, that we might be enabled, in future, to contradict this ridiculous report.

At ſix in the evening the congregation aſſembled, and on our entrance into the chapel, we obſerved on the north ſide, from a ſort of ſtage or pulpit, erected on the occaſion, a man, in appearance, a common day-labourer, holding forth to an ignorant and deluded multitude. Our entrance at firſt, ſeemed to excite a general diſſatisfaction; and our near neighbours, as if conſcious of their eccentricities, muttered bitter complaints againſt the admittance of ſtrangers. The chapel, which was not divided into pews, and even deſtitute of ſeats, contained near an hundred people; half way round was erected a gallery. The preacher continued raving, and, indeed, foaming at the mouth, in a manner too ſhocking to relate :—he allowed himſelf no time to breathe, but ſeemingly intoxicated, uttered the moſt diſmal howls and groans imaginable, which were anſwered by the congregation, ſo loud, as occaſionally to drown even the voice of the preacher. At laſt, being nearly exhauſted by continual vocifera-tion, and fainting from exertion, he ſunk down in the pulpit : the meeting, however, did not diſperſe; a pſalm was immediately ſung by a man, who, we ima-gine, officiated as clerk, accompanied by the whole

congre-

congregation. The pſalm had not continued long, before we obſerved part of the aſſembly, to our great ſurpriſe, *jumping* in ſmall parties of three, four, and ſometimes five in a ſet, lifting up their hands, beating their breaſts, and making the moſt horrid geſticulations. Each individual ſeparately jumped, regularly ſucceeding one another, while the reſt generally aſſiſted the jumper by the help of their hands. The women always appeared more vehement than the men, and infinitely ſurpaſſed them in numbers; ſeeming to endeavour to excel each other in jumping, ſcreaming, and howling. We obſerved, indeed, that many of them loſt their ſhoes, hats, and bonnets, with the utmoſt indifference, and never condeſcended to ſearch after them; in this condition, it is not unuſual to meet them jumping to their homes. Their meetings are twice a week, Wedneſdays and Sundays. Having accidentally met with a gentleman, at the Hotel, a native of Siberia, we invited him to our party, and, induced by curioſity, he readily accompanied us to the chapel. On the commencement of the *jumping*, he intreated us to quit the congregation, exclaiming, "Good "God! I for a moment forgot I was in a Chriſtian "country; the dance of the Siberians, in the worſhip "of the Lama, with their ſhouts and geſticulations, is "not more horrid!" This obſervation ſo forcibly ſtruck me, that I could not avoid inſerting it in my note-book.

With

With difguft we left the chapel, and were given to underftand, by our landlord, they celebrate a particular day every year, when inftances have been known of women dying by too great an exertion ; and fainting is frequently the confequence of their exceffive jumping.

This fect is by no means confined to the town of Caernarvon, but in many villages, and in feveral market towns, both in North and South Wales,* they have eftablifhed regular chapels. "They have" (fays a correfpondent to the Gentleman's Magazine,†) "periodical meetings in many of the larger towns, to "which they come from thirty to forty miles round. "At one, held in Denbigh, about laft April, there "were, I believe, upwards of four thoufand people, "from different parts. At another, held in Bala, "foon afterwards, nearly double that number were "fuppofed to be prefent." The laft number appears rather to be exaggerated, though the latter, being dated from Denbigh, fhould be confidered as authoritative.

Another correfpondent to the Gentleman's Magazine, gives the following information refpecting the fect : "That they are not a diftinct fect, but *Methodifts*,

---

* I have fince underftood, that they have a chapel at Caermarthen.

† September, 1799, p. 741.

"of

" of the fame perfuafion as the late Mr. Whitfield ;
" for though there are feveral congregations of *Wef-
" leyan Methodifts*, in this country, there is no fuch
" cuftom amongft them. But jumping during reli-
" gious worfhip is no new thing amongft the other
" party, having (by what I can learn) been practifed
" by them for many years paft. I have feen fome of
" their pamphlets, in the Welch language, in which
" this cuftom is juftified by the example of David,
" who danced before the ark ; and of the lame man,
" reftored by our bleffed Saviour, at the gate of the
" Temple, who leaped for joy." How far this gentleman's account may be accurate, I leave for others to
decide ; it is certainly to be lamented, in a country
where the Chriftian Religion is preached in a ftile of
the greateft purity and fimplicity, that thofe poor ignorant deluded wretches fhould be led to a form of worfhip fo diffonant to the Eftablifhed Church of England,
and, indeed, by a poor ignorant fellow, devoid of edu-
cation, and devoid of fenfe.

The fame road we had fo much admired the pre-
ceding Saturday, foon brought us to

BANGOR,

the fuppofed fcite of the Bovium, or Bonium, a Roman
ftation,

ftation, and celebrated for the moft antient Britifh
monaftery, which contained two thoufand four hundred
monks : it has long retained its Britifh name, *Bangor*,
or *Bancher*, fignifying " a beautiful quire ;" an appellation it juftly merits.   The fituation is deeply fe-
cluded, " far from the buftle of a jarring world," and
muft have accorded well with monaftic melancholy;
for the Monks, emerging from their retired cells,
might here indulge in that luxurious melancholy,
which the profpect infpires, and which would footh
the afperities which the fevere difcipline of fuperftition
inflicted on them.   The fituation of Banchor appears
more like a fcene of airy enchantment, than reality,
and the refidences of the canons are endeared to the
votaries of landfcape by the profpect they command.
On the oppofite fhore, the town of Beaumaris is ftraggling up the fteep declivity, with its quay crowded
with veffels, and all appeared buftle and confufion;
the contraft which the nearer profpect infpired, was
too evident to efcape our notice, where the

> Oak, whofe boughs were mofs'd with age,
> And high top bald with dry antiquity,

afforded a feat for the contemplation of the wide expanfe of the ocean, which is feen beyond the little
Ifland of Puffin, or Prieftholm ; fo called, from the
quantity

quantity of birds of that species, which refort here in the fummer-months.

The cathedral has been built at different times, but no part very antient; it was made an epifcopal fee, about the time of the conqueft: the church was burnt down by Owen Glendwr, in the reign of Henry IV. the choir was afterwards built by Bifhop Henry Dene,* between 1496 and 1500; the tower and nave by Bifhop Skevington, 1532. The whole is Gothic architecture, with no other particular ornament to diftinguifh it from a common Englifh parifh church. There are, however, feveral bifhops† buried in the choir. I could dwell with pleafure on the picturefque beauties of this little epifcopal fee; but a repetition of the fame epithets *grand, beautiful, fublime, fine,* with a long catalogue, which muft neceffarily occur, would appear tautologous on paper, though their archetypes in nature would

* Or Deane.

† As from neglect we did not tranfcribe the names of the bifhops, it may not be deemed improper to infert the following paffage from a well-known Author: "Here are monuments for Bifhops Glynn, 1550; "Robinfon, 1584; Vaughan, 1597; Rowlands, 1616; Morgan, 1673; "and one with a crofs fleuri in the fouth tranfept, afcribed to Owen "Glendwr; but as he was buried at Monington, in Herefordfhire, where "he died, I fhould rather afcribe it to fome of the earlier bifhops; Mr. "Pennant gives it to Owen Gwynned."

assume

assume new colours at every change of position of the beholder. From this retirement, a ferry-boat soon conveyed us to

BEAUMARIS,

the largest and best built town in Anglesea, where the same busy scene occurred. Having taken a short survey of Baron Hill, the seat of Lord Bulkley, commanding a fine prospect of the ocean, with the huge promontory of Pen-mawn-maur, we were soon convinced, that there was nothing to require a longer stay; and returning to Bangor, we pursued the road to Conway. About two miles on our left, we passed the Park and Castle of Penrhyn, the seat of Lord Penrhyn: this has lately been considerably enlarged and repaired, under the judicious direction of Mr. Wyat. The entrance is remarkably elegant, resembling a triumphal arch. This mansion enjoys a boundless prospect of the ocean on one side, appearing but feebly restrained by a long tract of scarcely visible coast on the other; in front, the flat Island of Anglesea, the lofty Pen-mawn-mawr, and the extensive point of Caernarvonshire: whilst the neat Church of Landegai forms a nearer object for admiration. We soon reached the dark lowering promontory of Pen-mawn-mawr, about

eight

eight miles from Bangor, rifing perpendicularly, in a maſſy wall, to the height of one thouſand four hundred feet : huge fragments of ſhattered rock are ſcattered by the ſide of the road, and a wall, ſcarcely five feet high, alone protects a carriage from the ſteep precipice ; which, from the ſlightnefs of the foundation, has even fallen down in many parts. In this awfully ſublime fituation we remained for ſome time, aſtoniſhed at the bold protuberance of the rocks, which ſeemed to project their dark ſides, to augment the idle roar of the waves.

Purſuing a good turnpike-road, we ſoon came in ſight of the hoary towers of

CONWAY CASTLE.

An air of proud ſublimity, united with ſingular wild-nefs, characterifes the place. The evening was far advanced ; and part of its ruins were ſhining with the purple glow of the ſetting ſun, whoſe remaining features ſtood in darkened majeſty, when we entered this monument of defolation. Paſſing over a plank, originally the ſcite of the draw-bridge, we came into the outward court, ſtrongly defended with battlements ; from thence we examined the grand entrance of the caſtle, with ſeveral abutments projecting forward, ſimi-

lar

lar in ftile to Caernarvon.   On the fouth fide of the
court is the grand hall, meafuring an hundred and thirty
feet by thirty-two, with eight light Gothic arches, five
of which are ftill in good condition.   On one end is the
chapel with a large window, a beautiful fpecimen of
Gothic architecture.   It is founded on the folid rock,
by Edward I. in the year 1284 : the walls are from
eleven to fifteen feet thick : all the towers are defended
by fmaller round ones, projecting two or three feet
over, with a regular communication round the whole
caftle by galleries, on the fame plan as at Caernarvon.
The fteps are decayed and broken, and the loofenefs of
the ftones rendered a footing very infecure ; but, impelled by an irrefiftible curiofity, we afcended the moft
perfect tower, and an extenfive profpect prefented itfelf
to our view.   The foundation of one of the principal
towers, looking towards a fmall river, which here joins
the Conway, has lately given way, and torn down with
it part of the building ; the remainder now hangs in an
extraordinary manner.   The whole town is inclofed
within ftrong walls, and defended by a number of
towers, which communicate with the caftle by a gallery ; there are likewife feveral gate-ways, at certain
diftances.

   The antient Church next attracted our attention ;
but did not detain us long, as the monuments for
                                                        the

the Wynnes, are the only things worthy of inspection. From thence we surveyed the remains of the College, which in the reign of Edward I. was intended for the instruction of youth: it is now in complete ruins: the workmanship curious, with several sculptured arms. In this town is an antient house, built in the form of a quadrangle, by the Wynnes, in the time of Elizabeth, now inhabited by poor families. This house is adorned, after the fantastical fashion of the times, in which it was erected; the roof is singularly carved, and the front decorated with the arms of England, with several curious crests, birds, and beasts: it bears the date of 1585. The arms of Elizabeth are carved over the door, fronting the street.

The trade of Conway consists in the exportation of slate, and copper from the Llandidno mines, from whence the finest specimens of the Malachite copper is brought. The town and castle of Conway are seen to great advantage in crossing the river, which is here nearly a mile over, and at high water washes the walls of that massy ruin: in the middle of the channel is a small rocky island. We observed, from this situation, the two castles, called Bodscaleen and Dyganwy; the small remains of the latter stand on a high rock above the river; the former is a beautiful seat of the Mostyns.

K.   We

We were foon tranfported into Denbighfhire; an extenfive profpect of the ocean prefented itfelf before us, and we difcovered the mountains of the Ifle of Man, which could fcarcely be diftinguifhed from the clouds of Heaven, and the waves of the fea. In defcending a hill, about two miles from the neat bathing-town of

ABERGELE,

we obferved, on our right, two immenfe caverns, about half way up the mountain; they are called Cavern-ar-ogo, and run four or five hundred yards into the ground; but their real extent has never yet been afcertained with accuracy. From thefe mountains, vaft quantities of lime are fhipped for Liverpool, and many parts of England; they are faid to be inexhauftible.

Abergele, fituated on the edge of Rhuddlan Marfh, is a fmall neat town, of one ftreet, reforted to in the fummer-feafon for bathing. The fands afford excellent walking; in the evening we lingered on the beach for a confiderable time, enjoying the calm, but cheerful beauty of Nature, and inhaling the pure fea-breeze—for,

"The

———" The wind was hufh'd,
" And to the beach each flowly-lifted wave,
" Creeping with filver curl, juft kift the fhore,
" And flept in filence."———

MASON's *Garden.*

With pleafure, mixed with reverential awe, we trod Rhuddlan Marfh, fo celebrated in the annals of hiftory. Here the ill-fated Richard the Second was betrayed into the hands of Bolinbroke, and taken prifoner to Flint : here the famous King* of Mercia met his untimely death : here the Welfh, under the command of Caradoc, in the year 795, were defeated in a conflict with the Saxons, and their leader flain in the action. This memorable and tragical event is handed down to pofterity, by an ancient celebrated ballad, called *Morva Rhuddlan,* or the Marfh of Rhuddlan, compofed by the bards on the death of Prince Caradoc.

The ground we trod, connected with fo many events, revived in our minds, the memory of paft ages, a feries of hiftorical events came to our recollection ; events, that are now fo diftant, as almoft to be obliterated from the page of hiftory. Paffing over a bridge of two arches, thrown over the river Clwyd, we entered

* Offa.

K 2

RHUD-

RHUDDLAN,

once the largeft and moft refpectable town in North-
Wales. Walking over the ruins of the caftle, I
recurred, by a natural affociation of ideas, to the
times, when the Parliament-houfe, the halls, and courts
echoed with the voices of thofe, who have long fince
been fwept from the earth, by the unerring hand of death.
One folitary Gothic window is now only remaining, to
diftinguifh the old Parliament-houfe, where Edward the
Firft inftituted that famous code of laws, under the title
of the *Statute of Rhuddlan,* from a neighbouring barn;
and, what once contained the Parliament of England,
now contains nothing but bark for the fupply of a
tan-yard.

The old caftle is built of red ftone; it confifts of a
fquare area, ftrongly fortified with a wall: this court
we entered through the grand gate-way, between two
round towers: the oppofite fide correfponds. The
whole is encircled by a deep entrenchment, faced with
ftone on the river fide, with two fquare towers, one
of which ftill remains.

The road from hence to

ST.

ST. ASAPH,

affords a moſt rich and beautiful walk, extending along the celebrated vale of Clwyd. This rich tract of land, called, *The Eden of North-Wales*, extends in length about twenty-five miles, and in breadth about eight. The neighbourhood of Ruthin affords the beſt view of this vale: though it is by no means ſo intereſting and romantic, as the vale of Glamorganſhire, yet its high cultivation, and picturefque, but moderate height of the hills, riſing on each ſide of the river Clwyd, renders the ſcenery pleaſing: its chief produce is corn. Both theſe vales claim the attention of the traveller; and both have to boaſt of particular beauties. One mile from St. Aſaph, we paſſed, on our right, the elegant ſeat of Sir Edward Lloyd. We ſtill followed the banks of the Clwyd, and at the fartheſt extremity a light elegant bridge, of ſeven arches, with the dark Tower of St. Aſaph's Cathedral, riſing on an eminence juſt over it, gave a picturefque effect to the whole ſcenery.

The town itſelf is built on a hill, in one ſtrait line, with a few neat houſes. The Cathedral naturally demands attention: the inſide is remarkably neat and elegant, entirely Gothic, with the ceiling of cheſnut, and open ribs, like the ſkeleton of a ſhip: it has lately

K 3   been

been repaired by Mr. Turner, architect of Whitchurch, at the great expence of two thousand four hundred pounds. The monument of David ap Owen, Bishop of this diocese, was particularlyp ointed out to us. The Bishop's Palace has been entirely rebuilt by the present diocesan. The Choir consists of a Bishop, Dean, six Canons, seven Prebends, and four Vicars. There are no monuments in the church-yard, and few of any importance within its venerable walls.

St. Asaph receives its derivation from its patron, who established a Bishop's see here, in the year 590: but in British it is named *Llan-Elwy*, on account of the conflux of the Elwy with the Clywd. It is singular, that the Bishop's jurisdiction extends over no entire county, but part of Flintshire, Denbighshire, Montgomeryshire, Merionethshire, and Shropshire.

The tract of land extending from hence to

DENBIGH,

is extremely rich in wood, pasture, and corn, but very deficient in water; directly contrary to the rugged scenes of Caernarvonshire; the summits of whose mountains appeared still visible in the distant retrospect,

mingling

mingling with the clouds. About a mile from St. Afaph, we were particularly pleafed with an old oak, whofe arms extending entirely acrofs the road, formed a moft elegantly fhaped arch.

Denbigh, fituated nearly in the centre of the vale of Clwyd, is a well-built town, ftanding on the declivity of a hill. A large manufactory of fhoes and gloves is here carried on, and annually fupplies London with a vaft quantity. The ruins of the caftle, ftill remaining on a rock, commanding the town, are too celebrated in hiftory, and too cruelly fhattered by the ravages of war, to be paffed unnoticed. The principal entrance forms a fine Gothic arch, with the ftatue of King Edward the Firft its founder, above it, in an elegant nich, curioufly carved, encircled with a fquare ftone frame. No part of this caftle is perfect; but the huge thick fragments, which are fcattered in the moft extraordinary and fantaftical manner, feem to tell its former magnificence; and a prefent view of things, fuch as they are, with a retrofpect of what they originally were, fpreads a gloom over the mind, and interrupts the pleafure of contemplation; yet ftill, the fingular character of this ruin is particularly interefting. Maffes of wall ftill remain, the proud effigies of finking greatnefs; and the fhattered tower feems to nod at every murmur of the blaft, and menace the obferver with imme-

me-

mediate annihilation. Amongst these ruins we lingered till the whole was filvered by the pale rays of the moon. To form a conjecture, on the extent of its apartments, is now impossible; but it is thus, described by Leland, in his *Itinerary*:

" The caftelle is a very large thinge, and hath many " toures yn it; but the body of the worke was never " finished.

" The gate-houfe is a marvellous ftrong and great " peace of work, but the faftigia of it were never " finished. If they had beene, it might have beene " countid among the moft memorable peaces of workys " in England. It hath diverfe wardes and dyverfe port- " colicis. On the front of the gate is fet the image of " Henry Lacy, earl of Lincoln, in his ftately long " robes.

" There is another very high towre, and larg, in the " caftelle caullid the Redde Towre.

" Sum fay, that the erle of Lincoln's funne felle into " the caftelle welle, and ther dyed; whereupon he never " paffid to finifch the caftelle.

" King Edward the Fourth was befieged in Den- " bigh

"·bigh caſtelle, and ther it was paȼtid between king
" Henry's men and hym that he ſhould with life de-
" parte the reaulme, never to returne. If they had
" taken king Edwarde there debellatum fuiſſet."

The pariſh church ſtands within the walls of the
original town. Below the caſtle are the fragments of
an old church, which for particular reaſons, that cannot now be aſcertained, was never finiſhed : it contains
nine windows on two ſides, with a large and handſome
one on the eaſt.

The vale of Clwyd ſtill retains the character of luxuriant fertility ; about two miles from hence, in our
way to

RUTHIN,

" Denbigh, fair empreſs of the vale," with its tottering towers, formed a moſt beautiful landſcape ; whilſt the
neat little hamlet of Whitchurch peeped from among
the pomp of groves. At the ſmall village of St. Fyn-
non St. Dyſnog, this curious inſcription over a door,

    " Near this place, within a vault,
      " There is ſuch liquor fix'd,
    " You'll ſay that water, hops, and malt,
      " Were never better mix'd ;"

                                invited

invited the " weary-way wanderer," to partake of the
good things within : this inclined us to be better acquainted with the author of this *extraordinary* ftanza ;
and we intreated the Landlord to be our director to the
much-efteemed well of St. Dyfnog. Paffing through
the church-yard, and from thence through the paffage
of an alms'-houfe, we reached a plantation of trees,
with a broad gravel-walk, almoft concealed from day's
garifh light, by the thick foliage: this brought us to
the fountain, enclofed in an angular wall, which forms
a bath of confiderable fize ; and fo

> ———" far retir'd
> " Among the windings of a woody vale,
> " By folitude and deep furrounding fhades,
> " But more by bafhful modefty, conceal'd ;"

that the " lovely young Lavinia" might here plunge
into the flood, fecure from the intrufion of Palemon.
Many wonderful qualities are attributed to this fountain ; but it is more particularly celebrated for the cure
of the rheumatifm : the water has no peculiar tafte.
We returned by a fubterraneous path under the road,
which led to the pleafure-grounds, adjoining the feat
of Major Wylyn.

Several feats were beautifully difperfed on each fide
of the vale ; among which, Lord Bagot's and Lord
Kirk-

Kirkwall's formed the moft prominent features in the landfcape.

Ruthin is a large neat town, only divided from the parifh of Llanruth, by a ftrong ftone bridge: the fcite of the church is extremely pretty, and is a handfome modern edifice: here is a monument to Dr. Gabriel Goodman, Dean of Weftminfter, in the time of Elizabeth, and likewife a native of this place. A new gaol has lately been built here by Mr. Turner. The remains of the caftle, at the fouthern extremity of the town, are fcarcely worthy a moment's obfervation; and the fcite of the old chapel is now converted into a bowling-green. Owen Glendwr demolifhed this town by fire, September 20, 1400. In the laft century, the loyalifts fortified the caftle, and fuftained a long fiege in 1646.

We ftill continued fkirting the rich vale of Clwyd; but winding up a fteep hill, overlooking the whole of it, from one extremity to the other, we were reluctantly compelled to bid a final adieu to all its viftas, hamlets, fteeples; the whole profpect, glowing with luxuriance, feemed to affume frefh beauties, at this our farewell view: the cattle, which were grazing in the fhorn meadows, and beautifully contrafted with the ripening corn, appeared more animated; and we difcovered, or
thought

thought we difcovered, an additional number of villages, peeping from the woody fkirts of the floping
hills. From this point the vale is certainly feen to
great advantage. To give a ftill greater effect, a thun-
der-ftorm came rolling on; and the clouds were

 " Silent borne along, heavy and flow,
 " With the big ftores of fteaming oceans charg'd."

This ftorm compelled us to feek for a fhelter, in a miferable pot-houfe; but the civility of the landlady fully
compenfated for its want of accommodations. The
effects of the ftorm rendered the remainder of our journey much more agreeable, and the heat lefs oppreffive:
a dull, uninterefting road continued, till we arrived
within four or five miles of

WREXHAM.

The contraft was too ftriking to efcape our notice;
but having climbed a fteep eminence, the eye commanded an almoft boundlefs range of land; and the
faint colour of the hills, retiring in the diftance, was
beautifully combined with the mellow green of nearer
woods. The counties of Chefhire, Shropfhire, and a
confiderable part of Wales, were extended, like a map,
for our infpection; the town of Wrexham, rifing in
       the

the bottom, animated the fcene, with its noble tower, overtopping the numberlefs little fteeples near it. Clofe to the road, we obferved feveral coal and lead mines, and a melting houfe for forming lead into pigs; thefe works belong to Mr. Wilkinfon.

The dirty out-fkirts of Wrexham, by no means pre-poffeffed us in favor of the town, but viewing it more leifurely, we can fafely affirm, that it is not only the largeft, but the beft built town in Wales.

To the kind attentions of a clergyman in the neigh-bourhood of Wrexham, we are much indebted, and under his directions, we furveyed the lions with great advantage. Our friendly Ciceroni firft conducted us to the church, an elegant building of the reign of Henry VII. The tower is an hundred and forty feet high, and efteemed " a beautiful fpecimen of the " florid, or reformed Gothic, which prevailed about " that time;" all the figures and ornaments are well defigned, and ftill in high prefervation. The infide is not lefs elegant; it has lately been neatly repaired, with a good gallery and organ: the painted altar piece is well executed. On the left, facing the altar, is a very handfome monument by Roubilliac, to the me-mory of Mrs. Mary Middleton; both the defign, and execution, reflect the higheft credit on the fculptor;

the

the fubject is the laft day; at the found of the trum-,
pet, a tomb of black marble burfts open, and a
beautiful female figure, cloathed in white, appears
rifing from it, juft awoke from the fleep of death; her
form dignified; candour, innocence, and celeftial joy
fhine in her countenance, and gives it the moft feeling and animated expreffion: in the back ground,
an obelifk, fuppofed to be erected to her memory,
is rent afunder; above, an angel, enveloped in a
cloud, is pointing to brighter fcenes. In this church
are two other monuments, executed by the fame celebrated mafter, in memory of fome of the Middletons; their defigns, though ftriking, cannot be compared to his laft day. Our worthy conductor,
perceiving we were great amateurs of paintings, and
careful that nothing of confequence fhould be paffed
unnoticed by us, particularly wifhed us to examine the
performance of a young artift, then at Wrexham: a
copy amongft others, of a painting of Rembrant's,
taken by Mr. Allen, from a celebrated picture, in the
poffeffion of Lord Craven, was moft ingenuoufly executed; the fubject is an old man, inftructing a young
boy; the attention of the latter, moft admirably preferved; the head of the former, and the hand particularly, moft highly finifhed. Without any exaggeration,
this painting would do credit to the moft fcientific
painter, and be efteemed invaluable; it is therefore to
be

be hoped, from the hands of fo young an artift as Mr. Allen, that this performance will be difpofed of, where judges of painting may view it with a critic's eye, and recommend its merits to thofe who can afford to encourage induftry and ingenuity.

Our friend's invitation to his hofpitable parfonage, and agreeable family, was too kindly urged, poffibly to be refufed, and in our way to

MARCH WIEL,

we vifited the feat of P. York, Efq. The grounds and plantations, are very extenfive; and the bowery walk, while they afford refrefhing fhelter from a fummer's fun, allow partial views of the counties of Chefhire and Shropfhire; with the Weeakin and Brydyork hills: in fhort, through thefe groves

   " How long fo e'er the wanderer roves, each ftep
   " Shall wake frefh beauties, each fhort point prefents
   " A different picture; new, and yet the fame.

The tower of Wrexham, and the town itfelf, as occafion offers, is a nearer, and an additional charming object. In an alteration of the walks a few years fince, were difcovered below the furvace of the ground, the

the shattered walls of an antient castle; these fragments Mr. Yorke has left unimpaired, and they remain a momento of the vicissitudes of fortune. The entrenchments round the castle, and likewise the original scite of the keep, are still very apparent.

The house itself is very indifferent: Watt's dyke runs through part of the grounds. In a parlour opposite the garden, we observed some fine paintings of the Hardwick family. Mr. Yorke has dedicated another room to the royal tribes of Wales,* where the arms and lines of the descent, as far as they can be traced, are emblazoned and hung up.

In the coolness of the evening, our hospitable host, conducted us to the neat and elegant little country church of March Wiel, lately cased with stone; and in the year 1788, ornamented with a new painted window by Mr. Eginton, of Birmingham; the twenty-one compartments contain the arms and crests of the Middletons and Yorks, with rich transparent borders. This window is undoubtedly very elegant, but the subject in my own opinion, more adapted to a hall,

* Since our visit to this spot, Mr. Yorke has published a most excellent and valuable book, entitled, *An History of the Royal Tribes of Wales.*

than

than an ornament to a church window. The high
tower appears not in proportion with the body of the
church.

Deeply impreſſed with ſentiments of gratitude towards our Reverend friend, and ſenſible of his hoſpitality and kind intentions, we took leave of him early the
next morning, and purſued our route to

RUABON,

purporting to viſit Wynſtay Park, the much admired
ſeat of Sir Watkin Williams Wynne. On leaving
Marchwiel, a moſt delightful proſpect ſpread before
us ; in the retroſpect, the tower of Wrexham Church
brought to our recollection the views of Magdalen College Tower, in the vicinity of Oxford.

The park of Wynſtay is well ſtocked with red deer ;
excellent plantations; and the houſe is an elegant
modern ſtructure, but nothing in the inſide particularly
deſerving the attention of the traveller. In the grounds,
the chief object, worthy of inſpection, is a very elegant
obeliſk, now erecting to the memory of the preſent Sir
Watkin's father. The height is an hundred and one
feet; the baſe of it ſixteen, and the top nine, built with

L

free-

free-ftone, and fluted : round the top is formed a gallery, with a handfome urn in bronze, after an elegant defign, caft in London ; round the bafe of the column, are wreaths of oak leaves, in the beaks of four eagles, caft in the fame metal.   On the fouth-weft fide is a door, with a ftair-cafe within the obelifk leading to the top : we regretted that the key could not be procured, as the profpect from that eminence muft be extremely fine.   On the other three fides, an appropriate infcription, in Englifh, Welch, and Latin, is to be carved.

Through this park runs Offa's Dyke, thrown up by the great King of Mercia, from whence it derives its name, to check the irruptions of the Welch, mark the confines of each country, and give greater fecurity to his own.   It begins at Bafingwerk, in Flintfhire, and ends at Chepftow, in Monmouthfhire ; extending a line of not lefs than one hnndred and fifty miles, over rocks and mountains.   This great undertaking ftill retains the antient name of *Clawdh Offa*, or Offa's Dyke.

Paffing through the little village of Ruabon, fituated at the extremity of Sir Watkin's Park, a very interefting and picturefque country, compofed of rich vallies, and gently floping hills, prefented itfelf to our view ; and, at fome diftance, we foon caught a glimpfe of Chirk
Caftle

Caftle, a noble feat of the family of the Myddleton's, ftanding on an eminence. Four miles from Llangollen, we enquired for the wonderful

PONTCYSYLLTY,*

(pronounced *Pont y Cafulte*) or famous aqueduct, now erecting over the river Dee, and found ourfelves within half a mile of this great and aftonifhing undertaking. It is not yet finifhed; eleven pillars are already compleated, built of fandy ftone, which is dug on the fpot; they are fifteen yards afunder, and their height, from the bed of the river, one hundred and twenty feet: over the whole is to run an iron trough, fufficiently deep for barges of confiderable burthen. On the middle column is the following infcription:

> " The nobility and gentry of
> The adjacent counties,
> Having united their efforts with
> The great commercial intereft of this country,
> In creating an intercourfe and union between
> England and Wales,
> By a navigable communication of the three rivers,
> Severn, Dee, and Mercey;

* Enquire the way to this aqueduct at the turnpike, about four miles from Llangollen.

For

For the mutual benefit of agriculture and trade,
Caus'd the firft ftone of this aqueduct of
PONTCYSYLLTY
To be laid on the 25th day of July, M.DCC.XCV.
When Richard Myddleton, of Chirk, Efq. M. P.
One of the original patrons of the
Ellefmere canal,
Was lord of this manor,
And in the reign of our Sovereign
George the Third;
When the equity of the laws, and
The fecurity of property,
Promoted the general welfare of the nation;
While the arts and fciences flourifh'd
By his patronage, and
The conduct of civil life was improv'd
By his example."

    This wonderful aqueduct reflects great honour to the undertakers of fo admirable, as well as valuable enterprize; and, fhould their hazardous fcheme fucceed, the whole nation muft indubitably reap great advantages: feveral columns muft ftill be erected, before the level can be accomplifhed. It is forming over the moft beautiful and romantic part of the river Dee; a bridge likewife, not far from this fpot, adds confiderably to the beauty of the fcene. Wood, water, and floping hills, all combine to render this vale interefting;

feveral

feveral detached cottages, are fprinkled through its wooded declivities, and here and there a gentleman's feat, "embofomed high in tufted trees," makes a pleafing feature, in the fafcinating landfcape. Returning to the turnpike-road, a fhort faunter foon brought us to the romantically-fituated town of

LLANGOLLEN,

(pronounced *Llangothlen*) completely environed with mountains, with a high hill to our right, bearing on its narrow peak the fmall remains of Caftel Dinas Bran. The bridge, adjacent to the town, thrown over the rapid Dee, confifting of fix arches, and formerly efteemed *One of the principal Wonders of Wales*, by no means anfwered our expectations. Some difficulty, no doubt, attended its firft erection, as the foundation is built on the folid rock : it is now repairing.

The elegant defcription of the valley in the kingdom of Amhara, by Dr. Johnfon, is very applicable to Llangollen ; for " all the bleffings of nature feemed here to " be collected, and its evils extracted and excluded." Without a figh of regret, not like the difcontented Raffelas, I could here pafs the remainder of my days, " in full conviction, that this vale contains within its

L 3   " reach

" reach all that art or nature can beftow ; *I could* pity
" thofe, whom fate had excluded from this feat of
" tranquillity, as the fport of chance, and the flaves of
" mifery." Such is the enviable fituation of Lady
Eleanor Butler and Mifs Ponfonby, who thus veiled in
obfcurity have fitted up, in a true characteriftic ftile,
an elegant little cottage, at the weft extremity of the
town, fituated on a knole : the two rooms, which are
allotted for the infpection of ftrangers, are very hand-
fomely furnifhed ; the dining-room is ornamented with
drawings, the moft favourite fpots in the vicinity
being felected as the fubjects. The window commands
a profpect of the mountains, which awfully rife in
front. The ftudy, looking on the well-arranged plantations of the garden, was appropriately furnifhed with
a choice collection of books : we regretted, in the ab-
fence of the gardener, that we could not gain admittance
to the grounds. The vale of Llangollen, and this
enviable retreat, have been the fubject of much admiration both in verfe and profe ; and highly deferve the
praifes, which have been lavifhed upon it.

" Say, ivy'd Valle Crucis ; time delay'd
    " Dim on the brink of Deva's wand'ring floods,
" Your iv'd arch glitt'ring thro' the tangled fhade,
      " Your grey hills tow'ring o'er your night of woods ;
" Deep in the vale receffes as you ftand,
" And, defolately great, the rifing figh command ;
                                    " Say,

" Say, lovely ruin'd pile, when former years
  " Saw your pale train at midnight altars bow;
" Saw fuperftition frown upon the tears
  " That mourn'd the rafh, irrevocable vow;
" Wore one young lip gay Eleanora's* fmile ?
" Did Zara's† look ferene one tedious hour beguile?"

The bridge of Llangollen is thus defcribed by the elegant pen of Mr. Pennant:

" The bridge, which was founded by the firft *John*
" *Trevor*, bifhop of *St. Afaph*,‡ who died in 1357, is
" one of the *Tri Thlws Cymru*, or three beauties of
" *Wales:* but more remarkable for its fituation than
" ftructure. It confifts of five arches; whofe wideft
" does not exceed twenty-eight feet in diameter. The
" river ufually runs under only one; where it has
" formed a black chafm of vaft depth, into which the
" water pours with great fury, from a high broken
" ledge, formed in the fmooth, and folid rock, which
" compofes the whole bed of the river. The view
" through the arches, either upwards or downwards, is
" extremely picturefque."

Having fatisfied our curiofity, Dinas Bran, or Crow

---

* Lady Eleanor Butler.   † Mifs Ponfonby.
‡ Willis's *St. Afaph*, p. 52, 285.

Caſtle, next invited our attention, and having attained
the ſummit of a ſteep and craggy hill, commanding a
pleaſing view of Llangollen, we arrived at the ruins,
which creſt this precipice.　The remains of this caſtle
are now ſo trifling, that it ſcarcely repays even the en-
thuſiaſt the trouble of aſcending ; its appearance is by
no means pictureſque, not a tree to give effect to the
crumbling walls ; nor has time ſpared one of the towers.

It was formerly the reſidence of Myfanwy Vechan,
ſo celebrated in verſe.　The caſtle is built of the ſtone
which compoſes the hill, on which it is erected.　The
proſpect is very pleaſing.　Chirk Caſtle, Wynſtay
Park*, and many other ſeats of reſpectability, more
particularly conſpicuous ; great part of the vale, and
the meandering courſe of the Dee, may here be traced ;
whilſt the oppoſite hills are ſhelved off in an extraordinary and unuſual manner, reſembling ſo many walls,
or fortifications.　Having deſcended this ſteep eminence,
we continued our route to Valle Crucis Abbey, about
two miles diſtant from Llangollen.　It would be ad-
viſable for ſtrangers firſt to viſit Valle Crucis, and take
Dinas Bran Caſtle in their way back to their inn.　The

* From a ſecond ſurvey of my note-book, I perceive, when ſpeaking
of the houſe, I omitted mentioning that there are ſeveral family pieces,
both of the Wynne and Williams, worthy the inſpection of the connoiſ-
ſeur.　The houſe has been built at various times.

transmu-

tranfmutations of time are frequently ridiculous : the long aifles of this monaftery, which were once only refponfive to the flow-breathed chaunt, now repeat the rude diffonance of ducks, cows, and all manner of poultry. Inftead of thefe emblems of rufticity, the mind's eye is more accuftomed to appropriate thefe antique edifices to the midnight proceffion of monks iffuing from their cells, to perform the folemn fervice. Thefe neglected walls are too deeply-fhrouded in their melancholy grove of afh-trees, to be feen to advantage; an axe, judicioufly ufed, would be of fervice to the ruin, as the elegant window of the chapel is completely concealed by the luxuriant vegetation around ; ftill, however, a pleafing melancholy pervades the whole fcene. The abbey is beautifully fkreened, on all fides, by woody hills, which entirely protect it from the inclemency of the winter.

This ancient ciftertian monaftery was founded by Madoc ap Griffith Maylor, in the year 1200, and is fometimes called Llan-Egwifte, or Llanegwaft. In this vale is the pillar of Eglwyfeg ; but the country people appeared quite ignorant of its fituation. Returning to Llangollen, we purfued the turnpike road to the neat village of

CHIRK,

CHIRK.

For fome way we followed the ftrait and formal courfe of a canal, near this, communicating with the Pont-y-Cafulte; we again paufed to furvey this wonderful defign.   The vale, on our left, was indefcribably beautiful ; and over the whole was diffufed the purple glow of the even.   The profpect was compofed of the miniature parts of the immenfe landfcape we had viewed from Dinas Bran Hill, each of which we now contemplated feparately as a fcene.   The moon's checkered gleam befilvered the walls of Chirk Caftle, juft as we entered the Hand Inn, where, after the fatigues of a long walk, we met with excellent accommodations, when confidered as a village.

After breakfaft the next morning, we endeavoured to obtain admiffion to fee the infide of Chirk Caftle, but without fuccefs, though now only inhabited by fervants, who were peremptorily commanded to admit no ftrangers.   It is fituated on an eminence, furrounded by a park, and fine plantations, which are very judicioufly laid out; this elegant manfion has been in the poffeffion of the Myddleton family, ever fince the year 1614. Having gratified ourfelves with a furvey of this noble park, we returned to the Ofweftry road.   Leaving the
village

village of Chirk, we croffed a new bridge, of one arch, elegantly conftructed : near is another aqueduct, of confiderable extent, now erecting over this river and valley, which, though very inferior to the Pont-y-Cafulte, is ftill a great undertaking : it is feveral hundred yards in length, and the brick piers rife fifty or fixty feet above the level of the water. Near this is a rich coal mine, lately difcovered. From hence to Ofweftry, we traverfed a rich enclofed country, and enjoyed a fcene particularly pleafing : all the inhabitants were collected, to gather in the produce of the ripened field ; and

> " Thro' their cheerful band the rural talk
> " The rural fcandal, and the rural jeft,
> " Fled harmlefs."————

To the traveller and the poet, fuch fcenes afford an ample field for amufement ; but waving corn is ill adapted to the canvafs of the painter. About two miles from Ofweftry, we paffed through the little town of

WHITTINGTON.

At this place was fought the battle between Ofwald, the Chriftian King of the Northumbrians, and Pènda, the Pagan King of the Mercians, in which the former loft his life. An eafy walk foon brought us to

OSWES-

OSWESTRY.

Its only relicks now remaining are the ruins of a chapel, built over a remarkably fine fpring of water; to
this was formerly attributed the cure of various difeafes,
incident hoth to man and beaft; and though its mi-
racles have long ceafed, yet it ftill bears the name of
the faint.   The remains of the caftle, fuppofed to have
been built at the time of the conqueft, are now almoft
too trivial to be noticed.   This town was garrifoned
by the King, in the beginning of the civil wars, but
captured in June, 1644, by the Earl of Denbigh and
General Mytton.

In paffing through the town of Ofweftry, we noticed
the church, as being a very neat building; but either
from our own negled, or imagining it not to be antient, we did not infped the interior.   Ofweftry fuffered greatly by fire, in the year 1542, and likewife
in 1567.

" The chirk of St. Ofwalde (fays Leland) is a very
" faire leddid chirch with a great tourrid fteple, but it
" ftandith without the New Gate; fo that no chirch
" is there within the towne.   This chirch was fome
                                               " time

" time a monafterie, caullid the *White Minfter*. After
" turnid to a paroche chirch, and the perfonage im-
" propriate to the abbey of Shreufbyri. The cloifter
" ftoode in hominum memoria ubi monumenta mona-
" chorum. The place and ftreate wer the chirch
" ftandithe is caullid Stretllan."

From this place to

LLANYMYNACH,

a continuation of the rich enclofed country, fhewing
to advantage the agriculture of thefe parts, attended us,
till we reached the foot of the hill of Llanymynach.
From the fummit of this we enjoyed a moft beautiful
and boundlefs profpect, commanding the whole dome
of the fky: all individual dignity was overpowered by
the immenfity of the whole view, which confifted more
particularly of the rivers Virnwy and Tannad, joining
their waters with the Severn; the lofty water-fall of
Piftyll Rhaiadr—the Breddin hills—and the Ferwyn
mountains. The geological obfervations on Llanymynach hill, by Mr. Aikin, are fo accurate, that to
attempt any further defcription would be deemed highly
prefumptuous in me; I fhall therefore avail myfelf of
an account, fo ably delineated:

" The

" The hill of Llanymynach, is not only remarkable
" for the fine profpect from its top, it is ftill more
" worthy notice, as containing by far the moft exten-
" five *lime-works* of any in this part of the country.
" The lime of Llanymynach rock is in high requeft
" as a manure, and is fent by land carriage as far as
" Montgomery, New-town, and even Llanidloes : it
" fells at the kilns for feven-pence a bufhel, and from
" thirty to thirty-fix bufhels, are reckoned a waggon-
" load ; the coal with which it is burnt, is brought
" partly from the neighbourhood of Ofweftry, and
" partly from Sir Watkin Williams Wynne's pits,
" near Ruaben. The lime lies in ftrata, parallel to
" the horizon, varying in thicknefs from three inches
" to five feet; it is of an extraordinary hardnefs, with
" but little calcarious fpar, and few fhells, or other
" marine exuvial ; its colour reddifh brown, burning
" to almoft white. Between the ftrata of lime, we
" found a very tenacious fmooth clay, orange coloured
" ochre, and green plumofe carbonate of copper, or
" malachite. It was in fearch of this copper, that the
" Romans carried on here fuch extenfive works, of
" which the remains are ftill very vifible: they confift
" of a range of from twenty to thirty fhallow pits, the
" heaps of rubbifh from the mouths of which, abound
" with fmall pieces of copper ore, and a cave of confi-
" derable dimenfions, terminating in an irregular wind-
" ing

" ing paſſage, of unknown length, connected with
" which, are two air ſhafts ſtill remaining open, and
" the appearances of ſeveral others, now filled up : in
" ſome of theſe caverns are found, large and beautiful
" ſpecimens of ſtalactite. One of the levels was ex-
" plored ſome years ago, and in it was diſcovered a
" ſkeleton, with mining tools, and ſome Roman cop-
" per coins. The whole maſs of the hill, ſeems more
" or leſs impregnated with copper : whenever the ſur-
" face is uncovered, there are evident marks of the
" preſence of this metal, and the ſtones compoſing the
" rampart of Offa's Dyke, which encompaſſes two ſides
" of the hill, are in many parts quite covered with
" *cupreous efflorenſcences*. Between the village and the
" rock, paſſes a branch of the Elleſmere canal, which,
" when navigable, will add much to the value of theſe
" works, by rendering them more acceſſible to the ſur-
" rounding country, and may induce ſome ſpirited ad-
" venturer, to recommence a ſearch after copper,
" which, it is evident, was formerly proſecuted with
" conſiderable ſucceſs."

This deſcription of Llanymynach hill, we pro-
nounce from our own obſervation, to be ſo very accurate, that the length of the quotation will be readily
excuſed. Leaving the pretty village of Llanymynach,
ſituated on the banks of the Virnwy, we reſumed our
journey

journey to Welch Pool; the face of the country was pleasing, and we soon reached the Breddin hills, on whose summit a column is erected to commemorate the victory of Admiral Lord Rodney over the French, in the year 1782. Not far from hence, we passed a handsome aqueduct, admirably constructed over the river Virnwy, of great strength and stability. The vale of the Severn affords much picturesque scenery, and we at length arrived at

WELCH POOL

Quay, about three miles from that place; several vessels were lying here, which carry on a constant traffic with Worcester, and the towns situated on the banks of this noble river. Before our entrè into Pool, Powis Castle appeared on an eminence, immediately rising behind the town, and beautifully backed with a large plantation of trees.

Welch Pool derives its name from a black pool in its neighbourhood; its Welch appellation signifying, a quagmire or pool, and is one of the five boroughs in Montgomeryshire, which jointly send a member to parliament. The town is by no means neat; it stands on a low hill, and consists of one principal street; in

which

which are fituated the new county hall, and market-places. The Severn is navigable within three quarters of a mile of this town, and computed not lefs than two hundred miles from its juncture with the Briftol Channel. It is the great market for the Welch flannel, called *gwart*, or webb, prepared in many parts of Merionethfhire, and generally ufed for foldiers clothes. This trade, however, has of late been very inconfiderable.

Powis Caftle lies to the right, about one mile from Pool, on the ridge of a rock, retaining a mixture of caftle and manfion: it is built of red ftone, and originally contained within its walls two caftles : the entrance is between two round towers. There are feveral family portraits in a long gallery, meafuring one hundred and feventeen feet by twenty :* it was formerly one hundred and fixty-feven feet long, but an apartment has been taken out of one end.† The gardens ftill retain that ftiff formality, fo much in vogue many years ago ; but the curious water-works, in imitation of the wretched tafte of St. Germain's en Laye, are now

* The meafurement of this gallery is copied from former tourifts, as fome MS. notes taken on the fpot, relative to this caftle, and the places coming under our infpection, the two following days, have been accidentally loft.

† See Lord Littleton's Account of Powis Caftle.

M   de-

deftroyed. The profpect from the caftle is very extenfive, comprehending a view of Welch Pool, Vale, and
Freiddin Hills.

From hence to

MONTGOMERY,

the Ellefmere Canal accompanied us part of the way;
and at length, after a fatiguing walk, we reached the
Green Dragon, a fmall and comfortable inn. The
feite of Montgomery is very pleafing, on a gentle
afcent, and backed by a fteep hill, beautifully cloathed
with the rich plantations belonging to Lord Powis.
The town itfelf is a ftraggling place, and little to recommend it. The remains of the caftle are now too
trifling, to intereft the paffing traveller.

In the year 1094, this caftle was gallantly defended
by the Normans; but the Welch, at laft, finding means
to undermine the walls, took it by ftorm; and, after
putting the garrifon to the fword, levelled that fortrefs
to the ground. It was afterwards rebuilt by Henry III.
in the year 1221, as a check to the incurfions of the
Welch; but a fecond time razed to the ground by
Llewellyn the Great, Prince of Wales: it afterwards
became

became the feat of the Lords Herbert of Cherbury, and their anceftors, till reduced to its prefent ruinous condition by the civil wars.

The road to

BISHOPS CASTLE,

brought us through a very rich country; and on af-cending a hill, about five miles from Montgomery, a retrofpect of the far diftant mountainous coun-try of Wales, to which we were now bidding a laft adieu, irrefiftibly brought on a train of ferious re-flections. In a retrofpect like this, where the fubject and the fcene muft infpire ferious thoughts, fuch traces are not unpleafing; they tend to promote one general effect—the love of contemplation. We enumerated the little incidents which had taken place, indulging reflections on fcenes for ever paft:—we erected, on the fpot which we efteemed moft adapted to retirement, the vifionary cottage: our fchemes were inftantly arranged,—fancy fafhioned its ornaments, adapted its appen-dages;—and fancy will ever exceed realities. But all our air-built plans of future happinefs foon vanifhed:—and alas! when

M 2

" fancy

——" fancy fcatters rofes all around,
" What blifsful vifions rife ! In profpect bright
" Awhile they charm the foul : but fcarce attain'd,
" The gay delufion fades.   Another comes,
" The foft enchantment is again renew'd,
" And youth again enjoys the airy dreams
" Of fancied good."——

Bifhops Caftle is fituated in a bottom : we found
it a more extenfive place than we had any idea of ex-
pecting ; but being fhortly convinced, that there was
nothing particular to require a long ftay, and having
recruited ourfelves at the Caftle Inn, we haftened to
leave the town.   The road, for the firft feven miles,
continually dipped into fhallow vallies, well wooded,
affording curfory views, with many a fubftantial
farmer's habitation lurking amongft the trees.   At
length, a rich and noble vale, with extenfive woods,
on our right, animated with feveral gentlemen's feats,
and watered by an overflowing ftream, running immediately clofe to the road, accompanied us to

LUDLOW;

fituated on an eminence, in the midft of this moft
luxuriant country.   After the many indifferent Welch
towns which we had paffed through, fince the com-
mence-

mencement of our pedeſtrian excurſion, we felt our-
ſelves not a little chagrined at our uncouth appearance,
in entering ſo gay a place. The ſtreets are commodious, and the houſes and public buildings extremely
neat. The gravel walks round the caſtle are extenſive,
and command, at occaſional points, diſtinct proſpects
of the gentlemen's ſeats, in the neighbourhood, with
their grounds, and noble plantations. The river
Teme gives additional beauty to this faſcinating ſpot ;
the new bridge, recently erected a little below the
caſtle, forms likewiſe, from this ſpot, by no means an
unintereſting object ; add to this, at ſuitable diſtances,
the river, by means of dams, is formed into ſmall artificial caſcades. At the extremity of the town, is another bridge, ſeparating the counties of Shropſhire and
Hereford. Theſe walks were laid out in the year
1772, by the Counteſs of Powis, at a great expence.
The overſhadowing trees not only afford refreſhing
ſhelter from a ſummer's ſun, but are likewiſe a protection from the piercing winter's wind ; indeed,

—————" I cou'd rove
" At morn, at noon, at eve, by lunar ray,
" In each returning ſeaſon, through your ſhade,
" Ye reverend woods ; cou'd viſit ev'ry dell,
" Each hill, each breezy lawn, each wand'ring brook,
" And bid the world admire; each magic ſpot again
" Cou'd ſeek, and tell again of all its charms."

M 3   Towards

Towards the North, the mazy courfe of the Teme,
—Oakley Park, the elegant feat of the Dowager Lady
Clive.—The Clee Hills.—The celebrated Caer Caradoc, with the other eminences, near Stretton, terminating the view, prefent a moft fafcinating landfcape.
Towards the Weft, a combination of rock, wood, and
water, gratifies the warmeft wifh of fancy.

The Whitecliffe, oppofite to the caftle, and Hack-
luyt's Clofe, near the Leominfter road, are the two
other moft favorite walks; but that round the caftle is
reforted to, as the moft fafhionable promenade.

The town of Ludlow has been calculated to contain feven hundred and two houfes, and nearly three
thoufand five hundred and fixty-five perfons.* The
public buildings are, the Market-houfe, the Guild-
hall, the Prifon, called Goalford's Tower, and the
Crofs: the rooms over the latter, are dedicated for
the inftruction of thirty poor boys, and fifteen poor
girls; and the former, at a proper age, are appren-

* This eftimation is taken from " The Ludlow Guide;" from which
I have taken fuch extracts, as, I flatter myfelf, will not be unacceptable to the tourift. We dedicated two or three days to the inveftigation of this interefting town, and confequently, in thofe parts where
the Guide is defective, we have made confiderable additions; and more
particularly, when fpeaking of the church.

ticed

ticed out. The town enjoys no particular manufactory, but its chief trade confifts in the article of gloves.

The caftle, the palace of the Prince of Wales, in right of his principality, is now entirely in ruins, except Mortimer's tower, which was repaired by Sir Henry Sidney, during his prefidency: it is now inhabited by an old fervant of Lord Powis's, a very civil and intelligent man, who related, with the utmoft concern, the fad viciffitudes this caftle had experienced; he infifted on our entering the tower of his habitation, and afcending the crumbling ftairs, for a full difplay of the various beauties in the vicinity of Ludlow, he expatiated much on a valuable diamond ring, which he had difcovered *himfelf*, when attempting to drain a cellar; the infcription of Hebrew chara&ers, round the gold, within the ring, was interpreted by the *larned*, "A good heart;" this, and feveral coins of filver and gold, which were found at the fame time, are now in the poffeffion of Lord Powis: near the fame fpot, a number of fkeletons were likewife dug up. He next condu&ed us to a fmall room in this tower, to obferve an old ftone placed over the fire-place, with a crofs; the letters W. S. and the date 1575, engraven on it.

Over the South-eaft gateway, leading into the interior

M 4

rior of the caftle, are the arms of Elizabeth, Queen of England, and beneath, thofe of the Sydney family, with the following infcription :

> HOMINIBUS INGRATIS LOQUIMINI
> LAPIDES.———ANN, REGNI REGINÆ
> ELIZABETHAE 23.———THE 28 YEAR
> COPLET OF THE RESIDENCE
> OF SYR HENRY SYDNEY KNIGHT
> OF THE MOST NOBLE ORDER OF THE
> GARTER, 1581,

This caftle, founded by Roger de Montgomery, on a rock, in the North-eaft angle of the town, fuppofed to be in the year 1112, was confiderably enlarged by Sir Henry Sydney. Its antient Britifh name, *Dinam Lhs Tywyfog*, fignifies the *Prince's Palace*. The viciffitudes of war have frequently been exemplified in this caftle ; it has had its Lords and its Princes ; it has been plundered, captured, difmantled, and repaired, in thofe periods of civil warfare, which this unfortunate country, in former times, continually experienced. Philips, in " The Hiftory and Antiquities of Shrewfbury," during thofe melancholy troubles, gives fome account of this caftle. Some hiftorians affirm, that Edward V. and his brother, were born in Ludlow Caftle ; but others, not crediting this affertion, attribute their birth to Wigmore : certain, however, it is, that during their

minority,

minority, they here held their court, under the tuition
of Lord Anthony Woodville, and Lord Scales, till
they were removed to London, and foon after fmo-
thered in the Tower, by the command of their cruel
and ambitious uncle, the Duke of Gloucefter. Here,
likewife, Prince Arthur, the eldeft fon of Henry VII.
celebrated his marriage with the virtuous Catharine of
Arragon ; and in 1502, he here paid the debt of
nature, and was buried in the cathedral church of
Worcefter.

The account of the reprefentation, at Ludlow, of
Milton's celebrated Mafk of Comus, is thus mentioned
in the Life of that poet, prefixed to Newton's edition:
" It was in the year 1634, that his Mafk was pre-
" fented at Ludlow Caftle.   There was formerly a
" prefident of Wales, and a fort of a court kept at
" Ludlow, which has fince been abolifhed ; and the
" prefident, at that time, was the Earl of Bridgwater,
" before whom Milton's Mafk was prefented, on
" Michaelmas night ; and the principal parts, thofe
" of the Two Brothers, were performed by his Lord-
" fhip's fons, the Lord Brackly, and Mr. Thomas
" Egerton ; and that of the Lady, by his Lordfhip's
" daughter, the Lady Alice Egerton."

In the firft year of William and Mary, the prefidency
was

was diffolved by act of parliament, " being a great " grievance to the fubject, and a means to introduce " an arbitrary power, efpecially in the late reign, when " a new convert family were at the head of it."

The church next demanded our attention, the only one belonging to this town. The time of the foundation of this antient and elegant ftructure cannot now be ftrictly afcertained : it is fituated on an eminence, in the centre of the town. The fquare tower is lofty, and of very light architecture, but the upper part fuffered much, by the all-deftroying hand of Oliver Cromwell. The highly-finifhed ftatues round the battlements, are much mutilated, and many entirely deftroyed. On entering the church, fix light Gothic fluted arches on each fide, with four fimilar ones of larger dimenfions, fupporting the tower, are ftrikingly grand. Under the organ-loft, we paffed into the chancel, now only made ufe of, for the adminiftration of the facrament. This is a moft elegant building, with thirteen ftalls on each fide, fimilar, in ftile, to the generality of cathedrals; the feats of the ftalls, all of which turn back, exhibit fpecimens of curious workmanfhip, with ftrange devices, and ridiculous conceits. Some of the glafs painted windows are ftill in good prefervation; the large one, over the altar-piece, reprefents the Hiftory of St. Lawrence, to whom this church is dedicated, in

fifty-

fifty-four compartments. The other windows of the chancel are much mutilated, collected from different parts of the church, and several panes broken, by the unmeaning idleness of boys ;—regardless of these valuable relicks of antiquity.—In the side of the wall, near the altar, are two stone stalls, with a piscina opposite.

In this chancel is a handsome monument, erected to the memory of Robert Townsend, and his wife, with several figures of their sons and daughters carved round the bottom : over them are the arms of their family and connexions : it bears the date of 1581.

A modern monument to Theophilus Solway, Esq.

An antient one to Ambrosia Sydney, who died at Ludlow Castle. This lady was daughter to Sir Henry Sidney, who attained the important situation of the Presidency of Wales, in the year 1564. He died at Bewdley, 1584, and left this singular injunction to his executors : " that his heart should be buried at Shrews-" bury, his bowels at Bewdley, and his body at Ludlow, " in the tomb of his favourite daughter Ambrosia :" this order was punctually executed ; and the leaden urn, containing his heart, was six inches deep, and five inches in diameter at the top, with this inscription carved three times round it :

HER

HER LITH THE HARTE OF SYR HENRYE SYDNEY
L. P. *Anno Domini*, 1586.

For an engraving of this urn, taken from a drawing of Mr. S. Nicholas, fee the Gentleman's Magazine for September, 1794.

Another monument* to Edward Wetfon, and his wife, kneeling oppofite to each other.

In a fmall chapel, to the left of the chancel, are three very handfome painted glafs-windows, containing the hiftory of the Apoftles, in eighteen compartments: there is alfo a rofary.

In this chapel is an elegant marble tomb, to Sir Thomas Bridgeman, ferjeant at law. In this church is likewife buried Sir John Bridgeman, the laft prefident but one of Ludlow Caftle.   He was extremely rigid in his office: and one Ralph Gittins, who had probably experienced his feverity, compofed the following epitaph on him:

    " Here lies Sir John Bridgeman, clad in his clay;
    " God faid to the Devil, firrah, take him away."†

---

   * No account of the infide of the church is given in the Ludlow Guide.

   † Phillip's Hiftory of Shrewfbury.

A chapel

A chapel corresponding on the opposite side, contains the royal arms of Charles, and several old iron armoury.

Should the tourist find time to make any stay at Ludlow, several excursions in the neighbourhood, will prove highly gratifying. Oakley Park, the elegant seat of the Dowager Lady Clive, claims the greatest attention; it is situated about two miles from Ludlow, on the banks of the Teme river; just beyond this, is a seat of —— Walpole, Esq. About five miles is Downton Castle; the noble mansion, and fine walks of Richard Payne Knight, Esq. one of the representatives in Parliament for the borough of Ludlow. Being necessitated to leave this charming country by a particular day, we had no opportunity of visiting these celebrated, and much admired seats.

With regret we left the fascinating situation of Ludlow, and crossing Lawford's Bridge, we ascended an eminence, along a fine beautiful terrace, commanding a most charming, and pleasant country to our left, with the fertile county of Hereford, aboundant with orchards, which were all bending with the produce of the year. About two miles from Ludlow on the right, we paused to admire the delightful seat of Theophilus Richard Solway, Esq. situated on an eminence, and skirted by a rich plantation of wood,

towards

towards the West : it is called the Lodge. Descending into a bottom, a rich country, studded with farm-houses, soon brought us to the town of

LEOMINSTER,

or Lemister, consisting of one long street ; the Market-place in the centre, bearing a very old date, and likewise the church, are both deserving of the traveller's notice.   It is situated in a flat, and the country round it not particularly interesting.

From hence, a turnpike-road, shewing to advantage, the rich culture of the country, soon brought us within sight of the venerable cathedral of

HEREFORD,

backed by a sloping eminence just rising behind, and beautifully cloathed with wood.   Being under a particular engagement to meet a party at Rofs, to accompany us down the Wye the following day, time would not allow us to investigate this respectable city, so minutely, as it deserves.   Our observations therefore, were so cursory, that " The Hereford Guide," must
supply

fupply the deficiences in this part of our journal; this neglect, the tourift muft attribute to our delay at the engaging town of Ludlow.

At Hereford, we for fome time hefitated refpecting the hire of a boat to convey us to Rofs; but the exorbitant demand of the boatmen foon determined us to purfue the turnpike-road, and follow, as near as poffible, the courfe of the Wye. The orchards were overcharged with "bending fruit," and feemed to prognofticate a more favourable cyder feafon, than has of late been experienced. The retrofpect of the city, with its antient cathedral, formed a moft attracting view; and about three miles, a moft lovely vale, bounded by the hills of South Wales, arrefted our attention. A continuation of the fame fcenery of orchards, in which Herefordfhire fo peculiarly abounds, with the road continually dipping into fhallow vallies, attended us within five miles of Rofs, when, afcending a fteep hill, a view of that town, or, rather, of its far confpicuous fpire, broke in upon the repofing character of the fcene. This prefently conducted us to Wilton Bridge, thrown over the Wye, about half a mile from the town; and, leaving the caftle of Wilton to the left, afcended the town of

ROSS,

ROSS,

to the inn, fo celebrated as the original habitation of Mr. Kyrle; but more generally known by the name of "The Man of Rofs." The landlord feems rather to depend upon the cuftom of ftrangers, from this circumftance, than the accommodations the inn offers. On the bridge we paufed a fhort time, to take a view of the meandering Vaga, which here confiderably widens; feveral pleafure-boats, of various conftruction, were riding at anchor, and united to enliven the watry fcene, whilft its fmooth tranquil furface, reflected and reverted every object fituated on the bank.

The life and character of Mr. Kyrle has too often been infifted on, and too frequently celebrated in verfe, to be again repeated, unlefs to "point its moral to the "heart;" teaching us, that felf-approbation can confer an inward happinefs, fuperior to all worldly applaufe; for,

"What nothing earthly gives, or can deftroy;
"The foul's calm funfhine, and the heart-felt joy,
"Is virtue's prize."————

Such a buftle pervaded the whole town, of parties affembling here, for an aquatic expedition to Monmouth,

mouth, the following day, that with difficulty we obtained a fmall room : from this circumſtance, it would
be advifable for parties to fecure themſelves accommodations during the ſummer-months, a conſiderable time
before hand, fuch is the continued affemblage of parties
forming for the Wye : a boat likewife fhould be hired,
and by mentioning the number of your party, the landlord will be a proper judge, refpecting the fize. Strangers may pafs, with pleaſure, the greateſt part of a day,
in furveying the views in the vicinity of Roſs ; views,
which muſt gratify the moſt fuperficial obferver ; but
more particularly from the church-yard. A walk
through the latter place to " The Profpect," fo called
from the profufe variety of objects, in the beautiful, and
the fublime, which are prefented from this fpot. The
fudden burſt of fuch a collection of beauties, the eye,
indeed, cannot contain without gratification. The
river below bends itfelf, in the whimſical and fantaſtical
fhape of a horfe-fhoe : this fingular wind of the river—
the ruins of Wilton Caſtle—the luxuriant counties of
Hereford and Monmouth, and the beautiful Chafe
Woods, all combine to promote one peculiarly grand
and beautiful effect. To enter into a minute defcription of objects, fo various and extenfive, is impoffible :
in fine, to delineate the beauties of the Vaga, with all
its accompaniments, would be enumerating every object
that is intereſting in Nature. Having fufficiently pored

N over

over the view from the Profpect, a ramble through the meadows will next prove highly pleafing.

The fituation of Rofs, though exceedingly beautiful, has nothing in itfelf to detain attention: the ftreets narrow, dirty, and inconvenient. The caftle of Wilton, fituated on the banks of the Wye, was founded in the reign of Henry I.; it was formerly a nunnery, from whence the Greys de Wilton derive their title.

Early in the morning, we congratulated each other on the favourablenefs of the weather, and with good fpirits provided all the neceffaries requifite for our water expedition; the enjoyment of which depends much on the feafon. The hire of the boat to Monmouth, by water, is one pound eleven fhillings and fix-pence, not including ten fhillings for provifions for the men, who likewife expect an additional fmall fum, after the fatigues of the day. The boat, navigated by three men, will contain ten or twelve people, without any inconvenience, and is properly protected by an awning, from the heat of the fun. The diftance from Rofs to Chepftow, by water, is more than forty miles, which ftrangers occafionally accomplifh in one day; but this hurrying method will not allow them an opportunity of infpecting, with proper attention, the various objects which deferve to be noticed; and they cannot poffibly

find

find time to leave their boat, and climb the rugged, steep banks of the Wye, in search of views, which, though visited by the discerning few, yet merit the regard of every amateur of nature's landscapes: and here it may not be improper to mention, the boatmen, from laziness, too frequently suffer these most interesting spots to be passed unnoticed by strangers, merely to avoid the delay of a few minutes. Gilpin, in his excellent treatise, "The Observations "on the River Wye," thus analyzes, in the second section, the beauties of the "echoing Vaga," and divides its constituent parts into—the *steepness* of its banks —its *mazy* course—the *ground, woods,* and *rocks,* which are its native ornaments—and, lastly, the *buildings.* To this he might with propriety have added, its *echoes* —the *variety of views* from its banks—the fishing *coracles,* which are continually on the river; for all these contribute to form one pleasing and interesting effect.

We embarked on board our boat, a little below the town; and the first object which drew our attention, was the ivy-mantled walls of Wilton: the annual growth of the few trees which encircle it, will, in time, render it a more picturesque object; it is at present so sufficiently seen from the water, as not to require the stranger to disembark for farther inspection. A few yards below, we passed under Wilton Bridge, com-

muni-

municating the roads from Hereford to Rofs: it is an elegant ftructure, of feveral arches. From hence, for four or five miles, the banks are tame and uninterefting, and fo high above the river, as to prevent a profpect of the adjacent country; but a groupe of cattle, fome ruminating on the brink, fome browzing on the afhlings, which overhung the ftream, and others

———— " from their fides,
" The troublous infects lafhing with their tails,
" Returning ftill,"————

formed a " rural confufion." The velocity of the ftream fhortly brought us to that noble fcenery, about four miles from Rofs, which fo eminently diftinguifhes and conftitutes the beauty of the Wye; before us, the noble remains of Goodrich Caftle, crefting a fteep eminence, enveloped with trees, prefented themfelves; behind, the thick foliage of Chafe Woods clofed the picture. The happieft gradation of tints, and the livelieft blending of colours, was here confpicuous. On the right hand we landed on the fhore, in order to make a minute inveftigation of the caftle: it is certainly a grand ruin, and ftands on an eminence, naturally fo fteep, as to render it, in former times, capable of fome refiftance againft a formidable enemy. On our firft entrance into the ruin, we naturally indulged reflections on paft fcenes, contemplated the traces of antient fplendor;

dor; and connecting what remains, with what is deftroyed; we pondered on the vanity of human art, and the ravages of time, which exhibit, in this ruin, their compleateft triumph. The warrior, who ftrove to preferve its original grandeur againft the attacks of Cromwell, is buried in Walford church, fituated on the oppofite fide of the river, and feen from the caftle. The different parts of the building, bear evident marks of its having been erected at various times; from a feat in the caftle-yard is the moft advantageous fpot for furveying, in one view, the whole of this ruin : an octagon pillar, of light and elegant workmanfhip, is feen to great advantage through the gate-way, and adds confiderably to the magnificence of this antient pile : it now belongs to Dr. Griffin, of Hadnuck, the lord of the manor. To return to our boat : we took a different and more circuitous route, for the purpofe of infpecting the remains of Goodrich Priory, now converted into a farm. The chapel has experienced the fame viciffitude; and thofe walls, which formerly re-echoed with the chaunting of voices, and the folemn peal, now repeat the continued ftrokes of the flail; in many parts of the walls, the initials of names of perfons, who have long fince paid the debt of nature, and left behind no other memorial, are carved with characteriftic rudenefs, fhewing, to every paffing ftranger, the prevalency of that univerfal paffion—the love of fame. The Gothic windows, and

N 3 the

the crofs, erected on each end of the building, fhew
evident marks of its former purpofe. The boat ufually
meets the paffengers at another reach of the river; but
it is a plan by no means to be purfued; fince, by miffing
a circuit round the caftle, its different tints, and variety of attitudes, occafioned by one of the boldeft
fweeps of the Wye, are entirely loft. A fhort time
after we had taken our laft retrofpect of Goodrich
Caftle, the fpire of Ruredean church appeared in front,
juft peeping from among the woody fkirts of the Foreft
of Dean : a little below, Courtfield Houfe, belonging
to Mr. Vaughn, was feen, in a very picturefque point
of view, with the ruins of the chapel, forming the back
ground. In Courtfield Houfe, tradition reports, the
warlike Henry V. was nurfed; and in the church of
Welch Buckner, fituated to the right, in a noble amphitheatre, enclofed with rocks, firft embraced the
Chriftian religion. A bufy fcene, of craft loading and
unloading, and coals fhipping for various parts from
the quay at Lidbroke, prefents a picture of cheerful
activity, and forms a pleafing contraft to the quiet,
rich, and retired fpots, we had left behind us; fuch
fpots, as were well adapted to form the mind of Britain's glory—the virtuous Henry. The banks now
became richly clothed with wood, from the fummits
of the higheft rocks to the water's edge; and a hill in
front, called Rofemary Topping, from the mellow,

lux-

luxuriance of its fides, clofed the profpect. Almoft every fweep prefents a new object, to ftrike the admiration of the fpectator: the tranfitions are fudden, but never fo harfh as to difguft; even the contraft between the embellifhments of art we had juft left, and the wild rocks, which here exhibit nature in her moft ftriking attitudes, give an additional impreffion to each other.

We now reached thofe fine mafs of rocks, called Coldwell, one of which, Symond's Yatch, to the left, it is cuftomary for company to afcend, in order to view the mazy and circuitous courfe of the river, and the extenfive profpect around. The Foreft of Dean, the counties of Monmouth, Hereford, and Gloucefter, were extended before us, ftudded with villages, diverfified with clufters of half-vifible farm houfes; with many a grey fteeple, "embofomed high in tufted "trees." In painting the feveral views from this fummit, the happieft defcription would fail; the impreffion can only be conveyed by the eye. The river here makes a moft extraordinary winding round the promontory, and having completed a circuit of more than five miles, flows a fecond time immediately under Symond's Yatch. The whole of this mazy courfe may be traced from this eminence. From hence we difcovered a very remarkable polyfyllabical articulate echo, and we reckoned twelve diftinct reverberations from the

N 4

explo-

explosion of a gun, fired on this spot.   It is here again customary for the boatmen to impose on strangers, and if they can prevail on them, during their walk to Symond's Yatch, will take the boat round the circuit of five miles, and meet them at New Wier, in order that no time should be lost; but this laziness we by no means encouraged, and the whole course of this extraordinary and romantic sweep proved highly gratifying.   Goodrich spire, which we again wound round, presented itself; huge fragments of massy rocks which have rolled down from the precipices, opposite Manuck Farm, here almost choaked up the course of the stream. The changing attitudes and various hues of Symond's Yatch, lifting its almost spiral head high above the other rocks, as we receded and drew near it, supplied a combination of tints surprisingly gay and beautiful; and having accomplished a sweep of five miles, we reached, within a quarter of a mile, the spot where we began our ascent to this steep eminence.

The view, at New Wier, next unfolded itself; but a disagreeable scene here generally occurs, and interrupts the pleasure of contemplation: a large assemblage of beggars, men, women, and children, on the banks, bare-footed, and scarcely a rag to cover them, followed our boat, imploring charity; and several almost throwing themselves into the water, to catch

your

your money, which, every now and then, the big-
ger feize from the lefs. This idle crew fubfift on
the trifles they obtain from ftrangers; and as beggary
is their profeffed trade, if their wants are not fatisfied,
they generally add infolence, with an oath, to their
demands.

But I have omitted to mention, that before we
reached the New Wier, the fpire of Haunton on Wye,
crefting a hill at the extremity of a long reach, and a
fantaftic barren rock, jutting out from the green foliage which encircles it, prefenting itfelf bold and confpicuous, formed prominent and interefting features in
the landfcape : this is called " Bearcroft," receiving its
appellation from the very refpectable and learned coun-
fellor of that name. Several rocks indeed, particularly in this part of the river, are named by the
Council, who have long made it a practice of exploring
the rich and bold fcenery of the Wye, on their affize
circuit. Gilpin, confidering New Wier as the fecond
grand fcene on the Wye, thus defcribes it : " The
" river is wider than ufual in this part, and takes a
" fweep round a towering promontory of rock, which
" forms the fide fcreen on the left, and is the grand
" feature of the view.——On the right fide of the
" river, the bank forms a woody amphitheatre, follow-
" ing the courfe of the ftream round the promontory :
" its

" its lower fkirts are adorned with a hamlet, in the
" midft of which, volumes of thick fmoke, thrown up
" at intervals, from an iron forge, as its fires receive
" frefh fuel, add double grandeur to the fcene. But
" what peculiarly marks this view, is a circumftance
" on the water: the whole river, at this place, makes
" a precipitate fall; of no great height, indeed, but
" enough to merit the name of a cafcade, though to
" the eye, above the ftream, it is an object of no con-
" fequence. In all the fcenes we had yet paffed, the
" water moving with a flow and folemn pace, the
" objects around kept time, as it were, with it; and
" every fteep, and every rock, which hung over the
" river, was folemn, tranquil, and majeftic. But
" here, the violence of the ftream, and the roaring of
" the waters, impreffed a new character on the fcene:
" all was agitation and uproar; and every fteep, and
" every rock, ftared with wildnefs and terror." The
accuracy and elegancy of this defcription, drawn by fo
mafterly a pen, I hope, will amply compenfate for the
length of this quotation. The extenfive iron-works,
mentioned in this paffage, belong to Mr. Partridge.
Below the New Wier, a continuation of the fame rich
fcenery ftill arrefted our attention, and rocks and wood
feemed to contend, which fhould be moft confpicuous;
till the winding of the river, round Doward's Rock, on
which was formerly a Roman ftation, brought us under
the

the houfe of Mr. Hatley, which commands a view of the river as far as Monmouth, when it is terminated by the town, and bridge of fix arches. As we drew near

MONMOUTH,

the houfe of Dr. Griffins, fituated on an eminence, and a banqueting room, erected by the inhabitants of the place, appeared above the town, on the left.

The town of Monmouth lies too low, to form a grand appearance from the water, but is, in itfelf, neat and well-built, and pleafantly fituated on the banks of the Wye.

As we repaired to our inn, we were both involuntarily led to take a retrofpect of the paft amufements of the day. The partial gleams of funfhine had given additional tints to the rich and bold fcenery, and every thing had confpired to render it a moft interefting aquatic excurfion. The variety of fcenes which Claude would have felected, had he now exifted, for his canvas; with rapture, too, would he have caught the tints; and, with the happieft effect, combined the objects into a picture, kept up our attention, and removed

moved that monotony which too often accompanies water excurſions.   Such has been the pleaſure of our firſt day's water expedition ; and, from the impreſſion it made on us, we eagerly look forward to ſome future period, when we may again retrace views, which memory will ever hold dear, and the pleaſure be then redoubled, with the remembrance of paſt occurrences.

The evening we dedicated to the ſurvey of Monmouth.—Oppoſite the Beaufort Arms, the moſt convenient inn in the town, is the town-houſe, handſomely built, with a full length ſtatue on the outſide, facing the ſtreet, with this inſcription under it: " Henry the Fifth, born at Monmouth, Auguſt the " ninth, 1387."   On the birth of this warlike and virtuous prince, the charter was granted to the town of Monmouth : it is governed by a mayor, two bailiffs, fifteen aldermen, nine conſtables, two ſerjeants, and two beadles.   The caſtle now bears few veſtiges of its former grandeur ; and of the regal dome, ſcarcely a wreck has eſcaped, through the long lapſe of years, the ravages of time : where a mighty king once gave audience, and where vaſſals knelt, now aſſemble the animate appendages of a farm-yard.

Near the caſtle is a very antiquated houſe, now converted

verted into a fchool, the property of the Duke of Beaufort. To this town Wihenoc de Menemuc, or Monmouth, in the reign of Henry I. brought over a convent of black Monks from St. Florence, and placed them firft in the church of St. Cadoc, near the caftle, and after, in the church of St. Mary. It was among other antient priories, and feized by the crown, during the wars with France; but was reftored again, made denifon, and continued till the general fuppreffion, in the reign of Henry VIII.* From hence we walked to the church-yard; clofe to which is the room where Geoffry of Monmouth compofed his well-known Hiftory: this is now a day-fchool. Monmouth has likewife to boaft of a free-fchool, founded here, from the following curious circumftance: Mr. Jones, a native of Newland, being in diftrefs, left his parifh and went to London, where he engaged himfelf as fervant to a Hamburgh merchant, and proving trufty in his office, he was by degrees advanced, till at length he attained a fortune of his own; willing to prove how far the charity of his native place would extend towards him, in difguife, he applied for that relief, which he was enabled to fhew towards others, but his parifh taking no notice of him, referred him to Monmouth, and would not redrefs his pretended com-

* Tanner's Notitia Monaftica.

plaints:

plaints : the latter however, being more charitably
difpofed, relieved him according to his wifhes.   Having thus proved their generofity, he acquainted them
of his real fituation, and promifed to repay their kind-
nefs, by obliging them in any demand, they fhould
requeft.   On this, they folicited the foundation of a
free-fchool, which he immediately built, liberally en-
dowed, and which from that time has been well fup-
ported.   The walk to the Folly, we were informed,
would have afforded us fome beautiful and extenfive
profpects ; the whole of this information we fhould
probably have found true, but the evening clofing, we
were very reluctantly neceffitated to return to our inn.

Early in the morning we renewed our furvey of
Monmouth : the church firft demanded notice : it is
a handfome ftructure, but the infide offers nothing remarkable for the infpection of the antiquarian.   The
gaol, built after the plan of the benevolent Howard,
is fituated in a healthy fpot, and, in every refpect,
rendered as commodious and comfortable, as fuch a
place will allow, for the unfortunate inhabitants.
Monmouth, indeed, contains feveral good houfes, and
the neighbourhood is refpectable.   A bridge at the
extremity of the town, with the antient gateway, bears
every mark of antiquity.

                                                    The

The hire of the boat, from Monmouth to Chepſtow, is on the ſame plan as from Roſs to Monmouth, the diſtance being nearly equal. Nothing now remained, but to recommence our water excurſion; and we accordingly embarked a quarter of a mile below the town, where the river Monnow joins itſelf with the Wye; from hence Monnow-mouth, or Monmouth. The weather ſtill continued favorable for our ſchemes: the banks on the left, were, at firſt, low; but as we receded from the town, the ſpire of Monmouth in the retroſpect, with the Kemmin woods, riſing from a rock of great height, on our left, under which the river meanders, engaged our attention; and to our right, Pen-y-van hill, was the bold and rich ſcenery we enjoyed, on our firſt re-embarkation.

The ſame ſcenery of rock, wood, and water, which ſo captivated us yeſterday, ſtill continued, occaſionally diverſified by light veſſels ſkimming by our boat, and increaſing in number, as we approached nearer the ſea. The rude hail of the boatmen, as they paſſed, was re-echoed by the rocks, and the dingy white ſails of the veſſels, which ſoon diſappeared round ſome bold promontory, were particularly picturesque. Coleman's Rocks appeared alternately, mantled with underwood, and pointed crags; large fragments ſcattered in the river, here divide the counties of Monmouth and

Glou-

Gloucefter.   At Redbrooke Hills, the curling fmoke
iffuing from the iron-works, formed a pleafing-accom-
paniment to the fcenery, and the whole exhibited a
picture of induftrious labour.   Thefe works belong to
Mr. Turner : the wood and meadow land of White-
brook Hills, were finely contrafted with the bufy fcene
at Redbrooke.   From hence a long reach, with Fiden-
ham Chafe Hill rifing confpicuoufly in the front,
brought us to the village of

LLANDOGO;

diverfified with cottages, from the bafe to the higheft
fummit of the floping eminence.   This village is about
nine miles from Monmouth, and arrefts particular obfervation; here veffels of confiderable burden were
loading with iron, and other commodities, for various
ports.   The appearance of the river, here, changed ;
the tranflucent ftream, which had hitherto alternately
reflected, as in a mirror, the awful projection of the
rocks, and the foft flowery verdure of its banks, was
affected, by the influence of the tide, and rendered
turbid and unpleafant to the fight.

A turn of the river foon brought us to the village of

TIN-

TINTERN:

we here obferved the ruins of an old manfion, belonging to Mr. Farmer, of Monmouth; this houfe appears
of an old date, and might probably claim the attention
of the curious antiquary, was he not fo wrapt up in
contemplating the venerable Abbey, which prefents its
Gothic pile, in folemn majefty. This auguft building,
great in ruins, and awfully grand in appearance, impels
the ftranger, as it were, imperceptibly, to land and
infpect its noble arches, its tottering pillars, and its
highly finifhed windows; the fpecimens of antient
architecture, which formerly were delicately wrought
by the hand of art, are now finely decked by that of nature. On our firft entrance, our attention was too
much engroffed, to exchange the mutual communication of thought; but the care which has been officioufly taken to remove every fragment, lying fcattered through the immenfe area of the fabric, and the
fmoothnefs of the fhorn grafs, which no fcythe fhould
have dared to clip, in a great meafure perverts the character of the ruin: thefe circumftances but ill accord
with the mutilated walls of an antient ruin, which has
braved the pitilefs ftorms of fo many centuries. In
this refpect, we by no means agreed with Gilpin, who

O   thus

thus defcribes it : " We excufe—perhaps we approve
" —the neatnefs that is introduced within. It *may*
" add to the *beauty* of the fcene—to its *novelty* it un-
" doubtedly *does*." But when this difguft was a little
abated, we indulged thofe reflections, which fcenes of
antient grandeur naturally recall.

This beautiful ruin is cruciform, meafuring two
hundred and thirty feet in length, and thirty-three in
breadth ; the tranfept ftretches north and fouth, one
hundred and fixty feet.* This ciftertian abbey was
founded by Walter de Clare, in the year 1131, and
dedicated to St. Mary, in the reign of Henry VIII. It
experienced the fame fate with many other monafteries,
and was granted, at its diffolution, to the Earl of
Worcefter, in the year 1537.

As we receded from the banks, Tintern Abbey,
with the Gothic fret-work of the eaftern window,
feemingly bound together by the treillage of ivy, appeared in the moft pleafing point of view ; floping hills
and rich woods forming a fine back-ground. As we
drew nearer

* WARNER's *Firft Walk.*

CHEP-

CHEPSTOW,

fome moft noble rocks, " nature's proud baftions,"
opened upon us, to the left, grander than any we had
hitherto admired, and which, we had previoufly determined, were inconceivably fine, and furpaffed any idea
we had formed of the channel of this romantic river:
to add to the magnificence of the whole, the fetting
fun tinged the rocks with the moft refplendent colours,
and the dewy frefhnefs of the evening improved the
charm of the fcene; the one enchanting the fenfe, the
other refrefhing it. The lofty Wine Cliff, to the
right, and Piercefield, with the curious projecting
rocks, called the Twelve Apoftles, and Peter's Thumb,
heighten, to the very extent of beauty, this noble fcene,
gratifying, beyond meafure, to the admirer of nature.
Another reach brought us in fight of Chepftow Caftle,
on a prominent rock, of which it feemed to form a part;
noble in fituation, and grand in appearance. The
fingular conftructed bridge, the rocks, and the fcarce
vifible town, here made a moft charming picture: this
we enjoyed exceedingly, but regretted a few more
minutes would fet us on fhore, and conclude our excurfion on the Wye; an excurfion which, the farther
we proceeded, the more we were interefted; and fo

O 2

much

much fo, as to determine a renewal of this pleafing tour, another fummer. The wooden bridge thrown over the Wye, at this place, is of very fingular conftruction; the boards forming the flooring are all defignedly loofe, but prevented, by pegs faftened at the extremity of them, from being carried away by the tide, and by that ingenious contrivance gradually rife and fall with it, which is here frequently known to rife to the extraordinary height of feventy feet.

Not having vifited the church, in confequence of the bad weather, at the commencement of our tour, we determined now to infpect it. The entrance, through the weftern door, is an elegant fpecimen of Saxon architecture, richly wrought, with three arches; in the infide is the monument of Sir Henry Martin, one of the twelve judges, who prefided at the condemnation of Charles I. and was confined in the caftle feven and twenty years.

A curious carved one to the Marquis of Worcefter and Lady, though not buried here; and another, of the date 1620, to the memory of Mrs. Clayton and her two hufbands, both kneeling.

This church originally belonged to the alien Benedictine

dictine priory of Strigule, but converted, at the re-
formation, into the parish church of Chepstow.

Admittance to the celebrated walks of Piercefield
can only be obtained on Tuesdays and Fridays. To
survey these with that attention which they deserve,
occupy several hours; the liveliest description cannot
do justice to the rich and bold scenery, with all its
accompaniments; the eye can alone receive the im-
pression, for,

   " How long so e'er the wanderer roves, each step
   " Shall wake fresh beauties, each short point presents
   " A different picture; new, and yet the same."

   " The winding of the precipice, (says Gilpin) is
" the magical secret, by which all these enchanting
" scenes are produced." At one point, both above
and below, as far as the eye can reach, rolls in majestic
windings, the river Wye; at another, the Severn,
hastening to meet " its sister river," is discovered, till
at last they are both lost in the Bristol Channel; at
another, these scenes are concealed, and thick woods,
apparently coeval with time itself, and a long range of
rock, burst upon " the wanderer," with irresistible
beauty and attraction. The occasional recurrence also
of the rude bench, overshadowed by some umbrageous
tree, and concealed from the steep precipice below, by

      thick

thick underwood, allow only glimpſes of the ſurrounding ſcenery.

The houſe has received great repairs, and elegantly furniſhed by the preſent poſſeſſor, Colonel Wood. Every apartment, indeed, has its appropriate embelliſhments.

I have thus brought my Tour to a concluſion; a Tour, which has been productive of much amuſement, and, I hope, not entirely devoid of advantage: it only remains, therefore, for me to add, that the Two Friends, having completed a pedeſtrian circuit of near eight hundred miles, parted with mutual regret, jointly exclaiming,

    " *Cambria*, as thy romantic vales *we* leave,
    " And bid farewell to each retiring hill,
    " Where fond attention ſeems to linger ſtill,
    " Tracing the broad bright landſcape; much *we* grieve,
    " That, mingled with the toiling croud, no more
    " *We may* return thy varied views to mark."

AD-

ADDENDA.

Page 44. The church of Tenby is a large, handsome, and antique edifice, and several monuments, bearing an antient date, worthy of notice.

On the left of the altar, is one to William Risam, with the following inscription:

> Two hundred pounds
> and 50 more
> He gave this towne
> to help the poore.
>
> The use of one on cloth
> and coles bestowe
> For twelve decrepid mean
> and lowe.
>
> Let 50 pounds to five
> be yearly lent
> The other's use on Burges'
> sonne's be spent.

On the same side, is a monument to the memory of John Moore, Esq. who, at the age of fifty-eight, and having by his first wife six sons and ten daughters, fell

O 4

despe-

desperately in love, which not being returned, he died
of a consumption, at Tenby: the following epitaph
is very allusive to his unfortunate catastrophe:

He that from home for love
was hither brought,
Is now brought home, this God
for him hath wrought.

Another monument to Morgan Williams:

Igne probatur
En animus rursus clare in corpore
Morgan Williams
descended from the heiress of
Robert Ferrar, Bishop of St. Davids
Burnt alive by bigots under Q. Mary;
was lately chief of Gargam
and senior in council at
Madras.
Where Oct. 27, 1690, aged 49 years
He resign'd the President's chair
and his breath together.
An employment of full 30 years
chronicles the continual
approbation of his conduct
particularly as
chief commissioner of the circuit.

SON-

SONNETS.

ADVERTISEMENT.

THE following SONNETS, the joint production of two Friends, were sent to the Author, as considered applicable to his Tour; it is therefore hoped, they may not be unacceptable to the Reader.

SONNET I.

TO FRIENDSHIP.

Addreſſed to the Companion of my Tour.

O BALMY comfort thro' this varied maze
Of life ! thou beſt phyſician to the breaſt,
With deep affliction's venom'd ſting oppreſt,
A thouſand arts, a thouſand winning ways
Are thine, to ſmooth the rugged brow of care,
And mitigate misfortune's keeneſt hour :
Yes, A——, partner of my Cambrian Tour,
Friend of my heart, how gladly do I ſhare
Thy confidence ; whate'er my part may be
Hereafter on this ſhifting ſtage of life,
This buſy theatre of jarring ſtrife,
May health and happineſs attend both thee
And thine !—on ONE, thy Heav'nly Guardian truſt,
Nor doubt protection—all HIS ways are juſt.

SON-

SONNET II.

The Contrast of Yesterday, and To-day; supposed to be written on the Summit of SNOWDON.

How gay was yesterday!—no storm was heard
To mutter round thy steep! yon sun arose
With golden splendor, and in still repose
Nature majestic thro' her works appear'd.
To-day, how chang'd!—loud howls the hollow blast!
The thin mists undulate! thy tow'ring height
Is veil'd in tempest, and eternal night!
So 'tis with man! contrasting prospects past
With dreams of future happiness—to-day
In gallant trim his little bark may glide,
On the smooth current of the tranquil tide:
To-morrow comes!—the gathering storms display
A sad vicissitude—the whirlwind's sweep,
Grasps at his prey, and whelms it in the deep.

SON-

SONNET III.

On leaving WALES.

WHY burfts the tear, as Cambria, now I leave
Thy wild variety of hill and dale,
Where fancy, fond intruder, lingers ftill?
Why do thefe parting fighs my bofom heave?
'Tis, that alas! I ne'er may view again
Thofe haunts, thofe folitary fcenes I love;
But thro' this vale of tears forfaken rove,
And tafte the fad viciffitude of pain?
'Tis, that I fadly breathe a warm adieu,
To long-loft fcenes of mutual amity;
'Tis, that I turn, my abfent friend, to thee,
" Think on paft pleafures, and folicit new!"
For thee my fervent pray'rs to Heav'n afcend,
And may we meet again as friend to friend.

SON-

SONNET IV.

To the Welſh Harp.

LOV'D inſtrument! again repeat thoſe ſounds,
Thoſe plaintive airs, that thro' my ſenſes ſteal,
With melancholy ſweet.   Their pow'r I feel
Soothing my ſadneſs, healing ſorrow's wounds.
Gently thou lull'ſt my ſufferings to repoſe,
Inclin'ſt my heart to ev'ry virtuous deed,
Removing from my mind each dark'ning ſhade
That clouds my days, increaſing all my woes.
Now ſwelling with the breeze, along thy vales,
Romantic Cambria! the ſtrain I hear,
Then dying ſoft away, comes o'er my ear
In whiſpers ſoft, ſtill wafted by thy gales!
Lov'd inſtrument! again repeat thoſe ſounds,
Soothing my ſadneſs, healing ſorrow's wounds.

SON-

SONNET V.

Suppofed to be written by Moon–light, on the Sea–shore, at TENBIGH.

I LOVE to mark the filver-curling fpray,
Juft kifs the pebbled fhore; the zephyr blows,
And ocean flumbers in ferene repofe;
While the moon's beams in quiv'ring radiance play
Upon its furface: yet ere long, that tide
May heave its foaming billows to the fhore,
And the fea boil in one tempeftuous roar.
See here thy picture, man! reafon, thy guide,
Can lull each guft of paffion into reft;
Her aid divine, her energy once loft,
In what a fea of angry tumults toft,
Raves the mad whirlwind of thy troubled breaft!
Blind paffion then can reafon's aid refute,
And degradate the man to worfe than brute.

SON-

SONNET VI.

On ſeeing LLANGOLLEN VALE.

O THOU, too captious of each airy ſcheme,
Fancy! thou dear deluſive traitor, ſay,
Are not thy charms the phantoms of a day,
That mock poſſeſſion, like a fleeting dream?
Here could I ſpend, if ſuch had been my lot,
Quiet my life; nor ſhould the ſhiv'ring poor
Depart unfed, unaided, from my door.
" Content is wealth," the emblem of my cot.
Here, by the brook, that gently babbles by,
Should ſtand my garden; there the bluſhing roſe
And woodbine ſhould their ſweeteſt ſcent diſcloſe.
But ah! farewell theſe dreams;—my big full eye
Swells with the burſting tear—I think, how few
The road to real happineſs purſue!

SON-

SONNET VII.

Prospect of Sun-rise from SNOWDON.

How grand the scene from this stupendous height!
How awfully sublime! the king of day
Flames in the east; old ocean's waves display
One globe of fire! one boundless flood of light!
With what unclouded lustre blaze the skies!
While * Mona's flats, ting'd with a golden hue,
Burst with transcendent beauty on the view;
And, Man, thy scarce seen mountains proudly rise.
Nature, beneath, seems prostrate! and my sight
Can hardly grasp the vast immensity!
Can then the muse attempt to sing of thee,
Nature's great God! Father of life and light!
Who bade the sun his annual circle roll,
Who guides, directs, and animates the whole.

* The Isles of Anglesey and Man, are discovered from Snowdon.

P

SON·

SONNET VIII.

To my Dog.

YES, thou haft been companion of my Tour,
And partner of my toils ! haft rov'd with me,
Thro' Cambria's rude and wild variety,
And often footh'd the folitary hour
With thy careffes ; yet falfe man can claim
Superior reafon, claim a mind endued
With love, with faithfulnefs, and gratitude ;
Love, a mere found, and gratitude, a name.
Yes, faithful creature ! and when thou art gone,
With fond attention fhall thy bones be laid,
And a fmall tribute to thy mem'ry paid,
In thefe few words, engraven on thy ftone :
" Here let in peace the faithful Sylvio lie,
" The trueft picture of fidelity !"

F I N. I S.

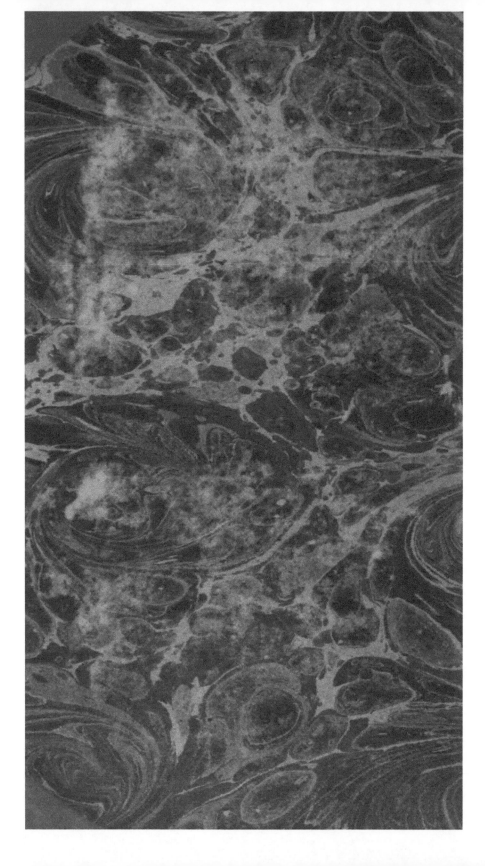

Lightning Source UK Ltd.
Milton Keynes UK
UKHW021011010520
362627UK00022B/2783